David Seaman
U.S. Democracy Promotion—The Case of Cuba

David Seaman

U.S. Democracy Promotion— The Case of Cuba

Budrich UniPress Ltd.
Opladen & Farmington Hills, MI 2010

A CIP catalogue record for this book is available from
Die Deutsche Bibliothek (The German Library)

© 2010 by Budrich UniPress Ltd. Opladen & Farmington Hills
www.budrich-unipress.eu

ISBN   978-3-940755-48-3

Die Deutsche Bibliothek – CIP-Einheitsaufnahme
Ein Titeldatensatz für die Publikation ist bei Der Deutschen Bibliothek erhältlich.

Budrich UniPress Ltd.
Stauffenbergstr. 7. D-51379 Leverkusen Opladen, Germany

28347 Ridgebrook. Farmington Hills, MI 48334. USA
www.budrich-unipress.eu

Jacket illustration by disegno, Wuppertal, Germany – www.disenjo.de
Printed in Europe on acid-free paper by

Contents

Preface

The United States . . . will oppose any attempt to weaken sanctions against the Castro regime until it respects the basic human rights of its citizens, frees political prisoners, holds democratic free elections, and allows free speech.

George W. Bush, July 2001.

If a post-Fidel government begins opening Cuba to democratic change, the United States . . . is prepared to take steps to normalize relations and ease the embargo that has governed relations between our countries for the last five decades.

Barack Obama, August 2007

They didn't elect me president to restore capitalism in Cuba, nor to hand over the revolution . . . We are ready to talk about everything, but . . . not to negotiate our political and social system.

Raúl Castro, August 2009

Addressing the prospects for a transformation in the United States policy of foreign democracy promotion under the new administration of U.S. President Barack Obama, Thomas Carothers (2009, 1) suggests that "the way forward for Obama will be more about changing *how* the United States goes about supporting democracy abroad than about *what emphasis* to place on democracy relative to other interests." The need for this change is a result of the Bush Administration's global crusade to promote freedom and democracy, which "badly tarnished" the U.S. agenda of democracy promotion "by relentlessly associating it with the Iraq war and regime change." As a result, Carothers continues, it caused many "to see it as a hypocritical cover for aggressive interventionism" and gave rise to "justifiable charges of double standards" (Ibid.). This book addresses one specific case in the Bush Administration's campaign to spread democracy: The case of Cuba. George W. Bush was certainly not the first U.S. President seeking to promote a democratic transition in Cuba. In fact, his strategies and methods were really nothing new. The U.S. Cuba policy has aimed at promoting 'regime change' through 'aggressive interventionism' for the past half-century. It is a policy that has provoked numerous 'justifiable charges of double standards' throughout its existence.

The research for this book began in 2008, during the final year of President Bush's second term in office. While this study focuses mainly on the Bush Administration's attempt to promote a democratic transition in Cuba, it also serves as a commentary on the long-standing U.S. attempt to promote political change in Cuba in general. During the course of the research, two pertinent, real world developments took place, which had the possibility of detrimentally affecting the timing of this study. The first event was the Cuban National Assembly's official appointment of Raúl Castro to the office of president in February 2008. The second, of course, was the election of Barack Obama as president of the United States in November 2008. To the fortunes of this author, neither development has greatly affected the state of U.S.-Cuba Relations and, thus, the central findings contained in this research.

Upon Raúl's election as President of Cuba, Western news reports immediately began speculating on the possible reforms which could potentially take place under his leadership. As the new Cuban president talked of the need to implement "structural changes" and address the "big questions" facing Cuba, *Newsweek*, for example, pointed to Raúl's "pragmatic nature," which may lead to important economic reforms, "opening up the economy to greater private investment and initiative along the lines of the Chinese model that he is said to greatly admire" (Contreras 2008). When he undertook positive, but minute, reforms in the social sphere by allowing Cubans to use cell phones, move freely in Cuba's tourist areas, and join in open public debates through a series of town hall meetings across Cuba, the *New York Times* reported that "the younger Castro's actions show he is willing to take Cuba in a different direction" (McKinley 2008).

In the United States at this time, Illinois Senator Barack Obama was in the midst of a presidential campaign. Before stopping in Miami, Florida to discuss his Cuba policy, he published an op-ed in the *Miami Herald*, faulting the Bush Administration for making "grand gestures" in promoting democracy in Cuba "while strategically blundering when it comes to actually advancing the cause of freedom and democracy in Cuba." The "best tool for helping to foster . . . democracy on the island," Obama stated, would be to loosen the U.S. embargo against Cuba by "granting Cuban Americans unrestricted rights to visit family and send remittances to the island" (Obama 2007). Shortly after taking office in January 2009, the new U.S. President followed through on this campaign declaration. On April 13, 2009, his administration announced that it was loosening restrictions on Cuban Americans regarding travel to Cuba and the sending of remittances and gifts to family members in Cuba – provided, of course, that none of these family members are in the Cuban Government or the Cuban Communist Party. In a further step, the president authorized U.S. tele-communications firms to enter into agreements with Cuban providers in order to establish wider telecommunications services between the United States and Cuba.

While some commentators expressed hope that these developments were the beginning of a new era, marking the end of the hostile nature of

U.S.-Cuba relations, others recognized that this hope was largely inflated. Akin to Raúl's domestic reforms, Obama's reforms in the area of U.S. Cuba policy have also "achieved only the minimum," as the Cuban President has pointed out (Weissert 2009). Indeed, to even describe these changes as 'reform' would be misleading. Rather, they are minor cosmetic adjustments within a set of already restrictive U.S. laws regulating these parts of the U.S. embargo, which the U.S. executive has the power to unilaterally influence. In the 1990s, U.S. President Bill Clinton first tightened, and then loosened, these restrictions. His successor, President Bush, again tightened them. And now, President Obama's loosening of the restrictions has brought the regulations back to where they more or less were under the Clinton Administration. This is not to say that the moves on the part of the Obama Administration are not positive. Indeed, a central aim, his administration states, is to "promote the freer flow of information . . . to the Cuban people" – an important aspect in any strategy to promote democratic change in a foreign country (U.S. Government, White House 2009). However, The problem runs much deeper than loosening restrictions for roughly 1.3 million Cuban Americans to visit family and send remittances and gifts to Cuba. The point here is that these changes greatly fall short of any real, deep-seated reform that can redirect U.S. Cuba policy in a logical way towards achieving its stated aim: the promotion of a democratic transition in Cuba.

As Mexican President Felipe Calderon remarked at the Trinidad Summit of Americas in April 2009, the U.S. economic embargo on Cuba "has been [in place] long before we were even born, and yet things have not changed all that much in Cuba" (Smith 2009). The following study aims at addressing this issue, not by providing prescriptive policy alternatives for the U.S. policy *per se*, but rather by identifying the underlying assumptions of, and the main instruments used within the policy, which fail to contribute to promoting democratic political change in Cuba. Identifying these mal-functioning structures is the first step in formulating any future policy that is geared towards contributing to the stated goal of bringing about a demo-cratic transition in Cuba.

The research presented in this book was undertaken in 2008 at the University of Osnabrück, Department of Social Sciences, in Germany. In addition to the numerous colleagues and associates who provided me with illuminating critiques during my research, I would particularly like to express my gratitude to Professors Dr. Roland Czada and Dr. Ralf Kleinfeld for their unparalleled assistance and encouragement throughout the research and its subsequent preparation for publication.

1. Introduction

Following the events of September 11, 2001, the administration of U.S. President George W. Bush placed democracy promotion at the forefront of its foreign policy goals. The administration's second National Security Strategy lists the promotion of freedom and democracy as "the goal of U.S. statecraft," which strives to "create a world of democratic, well-governed states that can meet the needs of their citizens and conduct themselves responsibly in the international system" (U.S. National Security Council 2006, 1). The strategy rests on the simple assumption that global terrorism is fueled by the lack of democratic institutions and norms in non-democratic states. The promotion of freedom and democracy, therefore, is seen by the U.S. Government as an inseparable component to winning the war on terrorism. Since this global war on terror began, however, the inconsistencies of the National Security Strategy in practice have come to light in many instances. Most notably, the contradictions can be found in the Middle East, where the Bush Administration has focused its front against global terrorism. Here, non-democratic governments like Egypt, Saudi Arabia, Pakistan, and the smaller Persian Gulf states have become indispensable partners in the administration's fight against terrorism, receiving increased amounts of military aid and economic assistance while simultaneously stalling on political liberalizations and failing to improve their human rights records.

Aside from buttressing these non-democratic partners in the war on terror, numerous other foreign policy interests can also be seen taking priority over promoting democracy. The desire for Russian security and economic cooperation, the addiction to Chinese economic power, and the search for reliable oil and gas reserves in Central Asia and the Caucasus – along with the investment opportunities awaiting U.S. energy firms in these regions – have triumphed any strong democracy promotion effort in these countries (Carothers 2007). As Paula Dobriansky (2003), Under Secretary of State for Democracy and Global Affairs, has stated: "No responsible U.S. decision-maker can allow our foreign policy to be driven by a single imperative, no matter how important. Thus, our policy toward a given country or region is shaped by a variety of considerations, including security concerns, economic issues, and human rights imperatives."

Although there are extensive examples in U.S. foreign relations where the promotion of democracy takes a back seat to more eminent, realist foreign policy objectives and thus gives certain authoritarian regimes an extended lifeline, there are also cases where the United States, seeming to have no great strategic or economic interests in a country, takes a hard line against non-democratic regimes, placing the demand for a democratic transition as its chief policy goal. Cuba, a small, tropical island 90 miles south of Florida, remains one such case.

The Republic of Cuba is a strongly centralized, socialist state with an authoritarian, single-party political regime established by the Cuban Revolution in 1959. The Cuban Communist Party controls the selection of candidates for election to the national legislature, the National Assembly of People's Power, as well as appointments to the top executive and administrative positions. Decision-making remains within the government and the party executives, while the National Assembly essentially serves only as a ratifying body (Bertelsmann Stiftung 2007, 3). Since Fidel Castro took power in 1959, it has been a policy goal of the United States to overthrow his regime and replace it with a government more compatible to U.S. interests. However, the various efforts of the past ten U.S. administrations, including invasion, sabotage, political isolation, economic coercion, and even assassination, have failed to bring down the non-democratic regime in Havana. Castro's continuous survival and his defiant attitude towards the United States has made Cuba one of the most "emotionally charged [issues] in American foreign policy," as Under Secretary of State David Newsom once explained (cited in Pérez 2002, 227).

The newest push to bring about regime change in Havana has come under President Bush, who, in the midst of his global democracy promotion program, assertively took up the Cuban challenge. While having greatly increased U.S. rhetoric for a democratic transition in Cuba, the Bush Administration has also strengthened the long-standing U.S. policy of promoting democracy in Cuba. On October 10, 2003, he established in his cabinet the Commission for Assistance to a Free Cuba (CAFC) with the objective of "exploring ways the U.S. can help hasten and ease a democratic transition in Cuba" (U.S. Commission for Assistance to a Free Cuba 2007; hereafter CAFC). Since then the commission has submitted two reports to the president totaling more than 500 pages of strategies and recommendations detailing how the United States can best promote a transition to democracy in Cuba. Coinciding with these new developments in U.S. Cuba policy, new developments were also taking place in Cuba. In July 2006, the 80-year-old Cuban leader temporarily handed power over to his younger brother Raúl Castro before undergoing intestinal surgery. In February 2008, Fidel Castro formally stepped down as President and Commander in Chief of Cuba and Raúl was elected as president of Cuba by the National Assembly. The transfer of power to Raúl, however, has done little to change the U.S. Government's strategy of promoting a democratic transition in Cuba.

The current U.S. policy can be seen as a two-pronged approach: Undermine the economic and political survival of the regime from the top-down while also strengthening opposition to the regime by promoting civil society activity from the bottom-up. The first prong, the objective of economically undermining the Cuban Government through a wide-reaching economic embargo, has now been status quo policy for a half-century. U.S. President Bush (2007) reiterated this top-down flank of the Cuba policy in September 2007 in a speech to an audience of U.S. diplomats and ambassadors, joined by several families of Cuban political prisoners:

America will have no part in giving oxygen to a criminal regime victimizing its own people. We will not support the old way with new faces . . . The operative word in our . . . dealings with Cuba is not stability, the operative word is freedom.

Regime change, as in the past, thus forms the main thrust of the U.S. Cuba policy and is to be brought about by destabilization through the creation of economic hardship on the island. In accordance, the Bush Administration has strengthened the embargo by clamping down on travel to Cuba and dollar remittances sent from Cuban Americans to the island with the aim of denying hard currency to the Cuban Government. This has been coupled with a determined effort to catch and persecute embargo violators.

The second prong of the policy, the bottom-up approach, is aimed at strengthening domestic opposition to the Cuban Government by means of promoting and supporting civil society in Cuba. By "empowering civil society," the State Department explains, "the United States aims to expedite a rapid and successful transition to democracy in Cuba" (U.S. Department of State and Agency of International Development 2007, 617). This approach is clearly grounded by the belief that the Cuban regime will collapse under overwhelming domestic pressure for democratic reform, as witnessed foremost in the popular uprisings in Eastern Europe during 1989 and most recently in the "color revolutions" that swept through Serbia, Georgia, Ukraine, and Kyrgyzstan. In his 2007 speech, broadcasted live into Cuba, President Bush emphasized the role of domestic pressure by urging the mobilization of popular opposition against the Cuban Government: "To the ordinary Cubans who are listening, you have the power to shape your own destiny" (Bush 2007). The strategy of funding civil society organizations – both U.S. and Cuban organizations – has most recently been stepped up by a four-fold increase of government funding, from $10.9 million in 2006 to $45.7 million for the fiscal year of 2008 (U.S. House of Representatives, Committee on Appropriations 2008, 2175).

Together, these two prongs seek to engineer the collapse of the current government in Cuba by pressuring from the top-down as well as from the bottom-up. Thus, in order to understand the efficiency of these approaches one must look into their underlying premises. These are two-fold. Firstly, the top-down strategy presumes that U.S. sanctions will bring about the economic ruin of the Cuban state and thereby facilitate a transition to democracy. Secondly, the strategy is based on the belief that civil society, existing within a closed, non-democratic environment, can be empowered from the outside and will subsequently bring about a transition to democracy. This policy approach raises important questions, not only for students interested in international relations and foreign policies of democracy promotion but also for those interested in democratization and political transitions, a discipline significantly enlarged over the past 20 years through an outpour of academic works.

To begin with, the absence of a diplomatic and economic relationship between the U.S. and Cuba and the hostility between the two governments over the last half-century has left the United States with virtually no remaining leverage over the Cuban Government to influence a political transition from the top-down (Sweig 2007, 40; Bremmer 2006, 76, 77). The overwhelming size of the stick – the punishing economic sanctions – has left no room to offer carrots, such as conditioned trade agreements, development aid or debt relief, which could possibly entice the Cuban regime to move towards gradual political and economic liberalization. A central aspect of this study, therefore, is to inquire into the relationship between economic stability, or instability, and transitions to democracy. In particular, the focus is placed on the efficacy of economic sanctions as a tool of democracy promotion that seeks to bring about democratic political change by instigating poor economic conditions. Indeed, in the face of poor economic conditions and decades-long U.S. sanctions, the Cuban regime has resisted any moves toward meaningful democratic reform, begging one to question the utility of the U.S. top-down strategy.

Furthermore, scholars have argued that, notwithstanding limitations, a strong civil society plays an essential role in transitions from authoritarianism to democracy (Diamond 1994; Schmitter 1997; Merkel/Lauth 1998; Paxton 2002). In the realm of democracy promotion, Diamond (1995, Ch. 2) has stated that external "aid to challenging groups in civil society (including groups in exile) is often the most effective way of pressuring for democratic change in a country with an entrenched authoritarian regime." To be sure, the democracy promotion strategy of aiding civil society within non-democratic regimes as well as in emerging democracies has increasingly grown in size and scope over the past decades. It is also a strategy to which the U.S. has given much credence as part of its Cuba policy, as displayed most recently by the $45.7 million the U.S. Congress has set aside for this task. Thus, a second aspect of this study is to inquire into the nature of the relationship between civil society and democratization and how the external promotion of civil society groups may interact within this relationship. Both the considerable degree of state control over civic organizations in Cuba (Bertelsmann Stiftung 2007, 10) and the precarious relations between Washington and Havana raise questions concerning the efficacy and consequence of U.S. assistance to civil society groups in Cuba.

Finally, the U.S. policy toward Cuba does not exist in a time warp, but rather it is situated within an historical relationship built by the past actions and reactions of both countries. Understanding the past helps greatly to explain the present, and without an understanding of the unique and volatile relationship shared between the two countries throughout the twentieth century, any analysis of the present U.S. efforts to promote political change in Cuba would be naïve and incomplete. Indeed, the intentions of the United States to bring the liberties of democratic self-government to Cuba reach far back into history to a time when the United States was setting the course of its Manifest Destiny – the consequences of which continue to retain their relevancy today.

By addressing these aforementioned questions, this study seeks to discharge the 'emotionally charged' issue of U.S. Cuba policy by means of a sober contribution to the debate. The following analysis of the goals and underlying assumptions informing the U.S. policy, as well as evidence of its operative efficacy, provides clear insights into the ineptness of the policy to promote a democratic transition in Cuba. The study is laid out as follows. Chapter 2 focuses on the development of U.S. democracy promotion in Cuba throughout the twentieth century. Not only does this historical analysis enable us to gain insight into the dynamics underlying the present U.S. Cuba policy, but it also touches upon the main historical perceptions informing the Cuban reading of this policy.

The study then proceeds to an in-depth analysis of the current U.S. policy. It is constructed so that the empirical analyses of both the top-down and bottom-up approaches are preceded by a general theoretical model of regime breakdown and transitions to democracy. This design allows for not only a clearer understanding of the assumptions underlying the U.S. policy, but it also provides an analytical framework for deductive insights into the malfunctioning dynamics of the policy. Chapter 3 addresses the theoretical underpinnings of the top-down strategy by looking into the relationship between a country's economic instability and democratization. This is followed by a brief discussion on the consequences of using economic sanctions as a tool to bring about regime collapse. Chapter 4 then turns to an empirical analysis of the top-down policy, probing the embargo's effects within Cuba's economic, political, and social realms, and, thereby, its impact on democratic political change.

At this point, the study moves to examine the bottom-up strategy. Chapter 5 looks into the theoretical relationship between civil society and democratization, and addresses the possible impacts of external interference on the internal dynamics of civil society relations with the state. Chapter 6 analyzes the U.S. program to promote civil society in Cuba. Here, two competing conceptions of Cuban civil society are presented with the aim of understanding which groups the U.S. recognizes as Cuban civil society and how these groups relate with the Cuban state. This is followed by a short overview of the U.S. programs to promote civil society in Cuba and the impact of this bottom-up strategy on the development of Cuban civil society. Lastly, chapter 7 provides an outgoing conclusion of U.S. efforts to promote a transition to democracy in Cuba.

2. U.S. Democracy Promotion in Cuba: The Historical Record

In contrast to the relationship of hostility and isolation that persists between the United States and Cuba today, the historical relationship between the two countries, much like their geographical liaison, has been quite intimate. No historical analysis of U.S.-Cuba relations can escape the theme of U.S. hegemony over the island. As Staten (2003, 3) suggests, it is the fate of Cuba so far that all Cuban leaders, whether Fulgencio Batista or Fidel Castro, have had to learn to "deal with and react to a powerful, hegemonic country," whether colonial Spain, the United States, or the Soviet Union. Following the birth of the Republic of Cuba in 1902, the United States came to exercise this hegemony over internal developments in Cuba. While this dominance was greatly weakened as a result of the Cuban Revolution in 1959, the U.S. has continued to maintain a position and policy that indirectly allows it substantial influence in shaping the framework within which developments in Cuba take place and future opportunities and choices are created. Likewise, due to this enduring and influential role exercised by the United States over Cuba, the historical narrative of U.S.-Cuba relations is also unable to escape the theme of U.S. democracy promotion, which, although not always apparent in observable behavior, has been recurrent in the official, public rhetoric used to justify U.S. policies and actions toward the Cuban republic.

Accordingly, this chapter lays out an historical account of U.S.-Cuba relations with a focus principally on the political and economic aspects of U.S. policy. It is essentially a narrative of the trials and tribulations of the Republic of Cuba to achieve and maintain a sovereign independence in the overwhelming shadow of its superpower neighbor and, likewise, the resolute endeavors of the United States to establish and maintain its position of hegemony over the island in order to better promote its interests. This historical narrative serves as a building block for any sober analysis of current U.S. policy toward Cuba that seeks to probe the efficacy of the strategies and tools used by the United States to promote a democratic transition in Cuba.

2.1. Endowing Democracy: U.S. Intervention in a Cuban War of Independence

The story of U.S. democracy promotion in Cuba began during a time when the young American republic was increasingly projecting its influence outwards. The United States had expanded westward across the North American continent, southward into Mexican territory, and, as the nineteenth century was coming to an end, it had further expanded its territory and influence out across the Pacific Ocean and into the Caribbean basin and Central America. The groundwork for this expansionism was laid out in a speech by U.S. President James Monroe to the U.S. Congress in 1823. In what became known as the Monroe Doctrine, the President issued a firm warning to European powers to keep out of the American continent, declaring that the United States would view any action on the part of Europe "to extend their system" to any part of the Western Hemisphere as "dangerous to our peace and safety" (Monroe 1823).

The Monroe Doctrine quickly became linked with the idea of a Manifest Destiny, a popular political catchphrase during the nineteenth century informed by ideas of racial superiority and national greatness. Manifest Destiny was seeped in a religious zeal symbolizing the destiny of Americans to spread their institutions of democratic self-government to those peoples less fortunate. By the end of the nineteenth century, the "Capstone idea" relevant to U.S. foreign policy, as Hunt (1987, 17) explains, "defined the American future in terms of an active quest for national greatness closely coupled to the promotion of liberty." This idea, intertwined with American notions that defined "other peoples in terms of a racial hierarchy" and a strong conviction that there were "limits of acceptable political and social change overseas," greatly informed U.S. expansionism (Ibid., 18). While the Monroe Doctrine condemned extra-continental intervention in the Western Hemisphere, it ultimately helped justify U.S. intervention into the internal affairs of the smaller Caribbean and Central American states. The Spanish colony of Cuba inevitably became caught in the clutches of this American Manifest Destiny.

Throughout the nineteenth century, aspirations of annexing the island of Cuba were regularly represented in U.S. political discourse. In the early 1820s Thomas Jefferson "candidly confess[ed]" to James Monroe in a private correspondence that he had "ever looked on Cuba as the most interesting addition which could ever be made to our system of states" (Peterson 1984, 1482). Jefferson was not the only U.S. president to have displayed such candid confessions; many others also shared this dream. In the decades to come, U.S. Presidents James Polk, Franklin Pierce, James Buchanan, and William McKinley all tried to purchase Cuba from Spain. But to no avail

Spain refused to let go of its colonial possession (Martin 1978, 14). When war broke out between the United States and Spain in 1898, however, the U.S. jumped to fulfill its ambition to bring its republican form of self-government to Cuba.

The Cubans had been fighting for independence from Spain since 1868, yet their efforts had proven unsuccessful against the colossal Spanish Empire. Following the outbreak of the second Cuban war for independence in 1895, a popular mobilization began sweeping through the United States in support of U.S. intervention to assist the Cuban people to freedom from Spanish colonialism. As the insurrection in Cuba dragged on, murder, starvation and disease began taking hundreds of thousands of lives and the agriculture and industry of the island was being devastated. On February 15, 1898 the U.S. battleship *Maine* exploded in the Havana harbor. Although the cause of the explosion was never satisfactorily explained, the blame immediately fell on Spain. The U.S. press, embroiled at the time in yellow journalism, made a frenzy out of the incident, pushing the American public into hysteria and thereby creating a ripe environment for those U.S. leaders harboring imperial ambitions. The incident was followed by a U.S. declaration of war against Spain, in which the U.S. Congress pledged to liberate Cuba from Spanish rule, while also taking care to assure Cubans that it had no "disposition or intention to exercise sovereignty, jurisdiction, or control over . . . [the] island" and intended to "leave the government and control of the island to its people" (U.S. Congress 1898).

In the United States, widespread popular support for the war was seen as a duty of moral righteousness to help the Cuban people achieve independence. One observer, writing for *The Century* in 1898, summed up the popular view at the time as he spoke of "a war of liberation, of humanity, . . . a war of disinterested benevolence" (cited in Pérez 1999, 357). The feeling was mutual in those U.S. congressional circles that were pushing for intervention "to aid a people who have suffered every form of tyranny and who have made a desperate struggle to be free," as one senator noted (cited in Ibid.). Yet the morally righteous declaration to help the Cuban people to liberty was not the only underlying motivation of the United States to intervene. Factors of economic and geostrategic interests as well as the desire for regional stability all played a role.

For U.S. agriculture, an 1898 editorial in *The Prairie Farmer* explained: "The real importance of the island to the United States . . ., stripped of all questions of sentimentalism, is its trade." Under "normal conditions," the editorial continued, "Cuba has been a large consumer of our agricultural products, and should be a much larger consumer of them than heretofore, with the establishment of peace and good government" (Williams 1972, 367). American business and industry, as a group of New York businessmen explained in a 1898 petition to U.S. President McKinley, were also suffering under the "loss of import and export trade" caused by the war, and in particular, were greatly concerned about the "heavy sums irretrievably lost by the destruction of American properties, or properties supported by American capital in the island itself, such as sugar factories, railways, tobacco plantations, mines and other industrial enterprises" (Ibid., 366). These concerns were made clear by McKinley (1898) in his war message to the U.S. Congress on April 11, 1898: "Our trade has suffered [and] the capital invested by our citizens in Cuba has been largely lost." "The right to intervene," he stated, "may be justified by the very serious injury to the commerce, trade, and business of our people."[1] Furthermore, Cuba was seen as an important strategic naval position to project U.S. influence and protect its growing trade and investments throughout the region.

Once the United States Navy and Marines mobilized against Spain, the war was over rather quickly. Spain ceded to the U.S. control of Cuba, along with Puerto Rico, Guam and the Philippines. Just as quickly as the Cuban war for independence ended following the entrance of the U.S., so too was the realization by Cubans that the U.S. had other intentions for Cuba than those pledged by the U.S. Congress. Cubans were excluded from the surrender negotiations and the following peace treaty with Spain. Then the United States took it upon itself to establish an independent Cuba by appropriating the Cuban treasury and setting up an occupation military government.

Ultimately the United States had no intention of granting Cubans absolute Independence. For the U.S. simply viewed the Cuban people as unworthy of this entitlement and incapable of the duties that go along with it. Firstly, the United States viewed the Cubans as an ungrateful beneficiary of its military intervention. The U.S. made no illusions as to who had won the war in its opinion. In the frank words of one U.S. congressman, "Cuba was given her liberty through the intervention of the United Sates" (cited in Pérez 1999, 359). Cubans, however, shared a different viewpoint. They had fought against Spain in two wars for independence and when the U.S. entered the second war in 1898, the Cubans had already greatly weakened the Spanish military effort, a factor that undoubtedly contributed to the quick U.S. victory over Spain. Furthermore, the continued presence of U.S. marines on the island did much to arouse Cuban suspicions as to what U.S. intentions truly were. As Cuban General Pedro Pérez explicitly put it in 1898: "The Cuban army has not fought for annexation or American control

---

[1]   In the last half-century before the war, the U.S. had developed close trade and business ties with Cuba, particularly in the sugar industry, Cuba's main export. By the outbreak of new hostilities in 1895, the capital invested by U.S. citizens in Cuba amounted to more than $50 million. The U.S. purchased 87% of Cuba's exports and U.S. goods accounted for 40% of Cuba's imports (Staten 2003, 36). According to U.S. President Grover Cleveland, trade between the two countries in 1894, a year before the war began, amounted to $103 million (Williams 1972, 334).

of our affairs . . . [but rather] for independence, and the army will not be satisfied with anything else" (cited in Ibid., 363). The United States seemed to have interpreted such adamant expressions of Cubans for a full, sovereign independence as evidence of ingratitude towards the U.S. intervention. U.S. popular opinion at the time greatly reflected this perception. After the United States entered the war against Spain, explained one popular newspaper, "the Cubans really took no further part in the struggle . . . The Cubans had done little more than help to consume the American rations, yet they were immediately ambitious to assume the reins of government and bid the Yankees good-bye . . . and have been more restless ever since, chafing under the restraint it was necessary to impose to save the Cubans from themselves" (cited in Ibid., 367). The *New York Evening Post* unabashedly concluded that "the Cubans themselves were not worth one gill of the good American blood spilled for their benefit . . . They are obviously a wretched mongrel lot, . . . ungrateful to the last degree for the condescension of the United States in coming to their relief" (cited in Ibid., 365).

Secondly, the perceived ingratitude of Cubans seemed to confirm the prominent, racist, and chauvinistic U.S. American view that Cubans were a people unfit for the freedom of democratic self-government. With "minds of no greater scope than children," posed a U.S. diplomat in Cuba, "how could they be expected to conduct successfully a Government of their own?" (cited in Ibid., 372). Likewise, the U.S. occupation governor, General Leonard Wood, described to President McKinley that the Cuban people are simply a "race that has steadily been going down for a hundred years into which we have got to infuse new life, new principles and new methods of doing things" (cited in Schoultz 2002, 400). "The political element," Wood explained in a follow-up letter to Washington, "appreciate only one thing, which is, the strong hand of authority and if necessary we must show it" (cited in Pérez 1999, 373). To be sure, it was precisely this strong hand of U.S. authority, which would be applied to promote the liberties of democracy on the Cuban island.

After 3 years of occupation the United States was prepared to turn over to Cubans their independence. It saw to it, however, that this independence would be controlled and regulated, thereby securing and protecting the growing U.S. interests on the island.[2] The U.S. designed Cuba's system of

---

[2]   During the U.S. occupation over 200 mining concessions and other economic perks had been granted to U.S. companies, so that by the time the occupation was over, U.S. investment had reached more than $100 million. By 1902, North American companies controlled more than 90% of Cuban cigar export trade and over 50% of cigar and cigarette manufacturing. The devastation caused by the war had left many Cuban business owners, farmers, and property owners unable to pay their debts or borrow capital for revitalization and were forced into bankruptcy. Accordingly, thousands of U.S. citizens moved in to purchase cheap property and land as its value fell dramatically. By 1905, 13,000 Americans had purchased land in Cuba (Staten 2003, 43).

self-government so as to restrict suffrage to only Cuban-born males over the age of twenty who were either literate, owned property valued at a minimum of $250, or had served in the military. These narrow restrictions eliminated the votes of two-thirds of Cuban males over the age of twenty (Schoultz 2002, 401). To ensure long-lasting U.S. influence over the internal affairs of the island the U.S. Congress drew up a list of conditions establishing the relationship between the two countries, known as the Platt Amendment. As a nonnegotiable condition to ending the U.S. military occupation, a Cuban constitutional assembly grudgingly adopted the Platt Amendment into the Cuban Constitution of 1901. Consequently, the resulting "independent and sovereign government of the Republic of Cuba," as the U.S. Government championed in the 1903 treaty between the two countries, displayed more the characteristics of a U.S. protectorate (American Journal of International Law 1910, 179).

The Platt Amendment strictly prohibited the Cuban Government from entering "into any treaty or other compact with any foreign power or powers which will impair . . . the independence of Cuba . . ., nor authorize . . . any foreign power or powers to obtain by colonization or for military or naval purposes, or otherwise, lodgment in or control over any portion of said island." The Cuban Government was prohibited from assuming or contracting any public debt larger than its normal ability to pay. By far the biggest detriment to Cuban independence, the Platt Amendment forced the Cuban Government to consent to the right of the United States "to intervene for the preservation of Cuban independence [and] the maintenance of a government adequate for the protection of life, property, and individual liberty." Furthermore, "to enable the United States to maintain the independence of Cuba, and to protect the people thereof," the Cuban Government was obligated to "sell or lease to the United States . . . lands necessary for coaling or naval stations" (Ibid., 179, 180).

At the end of 1901, Tomás Estrada Palma, a Cuban who had spent many years in exile in the United States and a strong supporter of the Platt Amendment, was elected as the first president of the new Cuban republic with backing from Washington. With the election of Palma, the United States had succeeded in bringing the pretense of democratic self-governance to Cuba. With the island now under the firm authority of the Platt Amendment, the U.S. occupation government packed up and returned to Washington. Before General Wood left the island, however, he wrote to U.S. President Theodore Roosevelt, insuring him that "there is, of course, little or no independence left on Cuba under the Platt Amendment" (cited in Schoultz 2002, 402).

The United States' intervention in the Cuban war for independence and its effective domination over the internal political affairs of the island would create long-term political, economic, and social consequences for Cuba.

Each country's popular interpretation of the events surrounding Cuban independence were difficult to reconcile. As Pérez (1999, 392) explains: "Americans expected gratitude; Cubans harbored grievances. North Americans remembered 1898 as something done for Cubans; Cubans remembered 1898 as something done to them." As a result, "the subordination of Cuban interests to U.S. needs produced national frustration and in the process contributed to the development of nationalist impulses driven principally by anti-American sentiment" (Ibid.). It was indeed these nationalist impulses, characterized by the underlying perception that Cubans had been robbed of their independence, which would fuel the events leading to the hostilities between Cuba and the U.S. a half-century later.

2.2. Paternal Democracy: Cuba Under the Platt Amendment and the Rise of Dictatorship

The Republic of Cuba would remain under the Platt Amendment until 1934. Ultimately, the Platt Amendment served to create the very instability in Cuba it was designed to hinder. As Domínguez (1978, 13) suggests, the United States' position of dominance over the internal political affairs of the island, rather than dampening the emergence of any viable oppositional Cuban politics and thereby establishing a strong and capable Cuban central government subordinate to U.S. interests, actually served to multiply the sources of political power so that no one group was able to impose its will on society for long. As oppositional uprisings and insurrections became the norm during the early years of the young Cuban republic, so too did the threat of requesting U.S. intervention – a factor that became the principle resource for political power in Cuban politics. Incumbent Cuban governments, facing revolt in the aftermath of fouled elections, were prone to ask Washington for protection. Likewise, any victory for the opposition was seen dependant on creating a crises situation large enough to compel the United States to intervene. Thus, the threat of U.S. intervention not only helped promote such insurrections but it also served to keep opposition politics alive (Ibid., 12).

This trend was clear within the first years of the new republic. In 1905, the fraudulent reelection of Cuban President Palma led to an armed uprising of the liberal opposition. As the insurrection grew and U.S. interests became threatened, U.S. President Roosevelt privately cursed to an acquaintance: "I'm so angry with that infernal little Cuban republic that I would like to wipe its people off the face of the earth" (cited in Schoultz 2002, 403). Publicly, however, Roosevelt responded by directing U.S. warships to

Havana, followed by the landing of U.S. Marines. Thus began the second U.S. military intervention in Cuba, the so-called "Cuban Pacification."

President Palma's government was forced to resign and a U.S. occupation government was established to 'pacify' and stabilize the situation. With the aim of promoting stability, the occupation government expanded the electoral system to include suffrage to nearly all adult males, established proportional representation in the Cuban legislature, granted several major public works contracts to U.S. firms to improve the county's infrastructure, and oversaw the creation of a standing Cuban army. This was thought necessary to provide political stability and protect U.S. economic interests, thereby reducing the need for the continued use of U.S. troops. The Cuban Pacification ended in 1909 with the election of Cuban President José Miguel Gómez and subsequent withdrawal of the U.S. Marines. However, it would not be the last time the U.S. troops were sent to intervene in Cuba. A racial uprising in 1912 prompted the U.S. to send in warships and troops to crush the revolt and protect U.S. property. And again in 1916, U.S. troops were sent back to quell an armed uprising that broke out after the fraudulent and violent reelection of Cuban President Mario García Menocal.

During the 1920s the Cuban public sphere was characterized by the growing popular demands of Cubans for an end to the rampant political corruption and the need for greater social justice. Furthermore, the continuous U.S. interference in the internal affairs of Cuba had contributed to a growing nationalism defined strongly by anti-Americanism within opposition groups. Rising unrest, which began playing out in the labor movements and among university students, came to a head in 1933 in an outbreak of violence against the corrupt and brutally repressive dictatorship of Cuban President Gerardo Machado. Once again, U.S. warships appeared in Havana's harbor. U.S. Ambassador Summer Welles was dispatched to Havana and the Machado government was forced to resign, upon which he and his cronies promptly fled to the Bahamas, taking the Cuban treasury with them (Staten 2003, 59). Washington sent in a U.S. military general to establish a temporary interim government and a deal was made to install a new Cuban Government under the leadership of U.S. favorite Carlos Manuel de Céspedes until new elections could be held. However, the U.S.-backed Céspedes government failed to gain support among the main groups who had fought against Machado's regime and proved inept at quelling the urban violence and acts of retribution that were now being carried out against Machado's supporters and members of his secret police. At this time, a military mutiny led by a young Cuban sergeant named Fulgencio Batista overthrew the Céspedes government and installed a revolutionary governing counsel under the leadership of liberal oppositional leader and university professor Ramón Grau San Martín.

Following the takeover, Welles reported to Washington that the revolutionary group was "frankly communistic" and incapable of forming "a government adequate for the protection of life, property and individual liberty" (U.S. Department of State 1952, 382; hereafter USDOS). For these reasons he recommended that Washington "not even . . . consider recognizing any government of this character" (Ibid., 390). As Batista continued consolidating his power within the Cuban military, the United States came to see him as the only authority in Cuba capable of preserving stability. After winning assurances from Batista, the U.S. began working with him to push out the Grau government and install an administration more aligned with U.S. interests. Batista swiftly forced the resignation of Grau and his supporters and a new government was formed under Carlos Mendieta. Real power, however, remained with Batista.

With the strong authority of Batista and his military to protect U.S. interests in Cuba, the United States finally abrogated the Platt Amendment, a move that also complemented U.S. President Franklin D. Roosevelt's Good Neighbor policy. As new Cuban governments publicly came and went over the next years, Batista's behind the scenes shadow government insured U.S. friendly policies and a degree of political stability. Batista himself served as president during the 1940s and proved to be a favorable strategic partner to the United States during World War II. After ending his term, Fulgencio Batista, now a very wealthy man through his power and corruption, relocated to Florida for several years before returning to Havana with aspirations of a second presidential term. As Staten (2003, 69) notes, the return of Batista to Cuba and his subsequent coup d'état in March 1952 "marked the end of all hope for democracy in Cuba and ushered in a new era that would have unforeseen consequences for Cuba, the United States and the world."

Since 1898 the United States had been engaged in promoting its brand of democracy in Cuba. Ultimately, it was a system in which U.S. paternal control over Cuban political affairs triumphed any development of independent and sovereign Cuban politics that may have encouraged the emergence of a stable and democratic political system. U.S. policy makers continued to hold no illusions as to democratic prospects in Cuba. Rather, as in the heyday of 1898, many still held the racist and chauvinistic view that Cubans were unfit for democratic government. This thinking was highlighted by one post-World War II U.S. ambassador to Cuba, Henry Norweb: Cubans "combine the worst characteristics of the unfortunate admixture of interpenetration of Spanish and Negro cultures – laziness, cruelty, inconstancy, irresponsibility, and inbred dishonesty." "Nine out of ten Cuban party leaders, Senators, Representatives, and principal journalists," Norweb believed, "would fit better into a Rogues' Gallery than a roster of responsible public servants" (cited in Schoultz 2002, 413). In general, the United

States' Latin American policy by this time had oriented itself to the fanatical Cold War doctrine of containing communism. U.S. postwar administrations were increasingly seeing 'red' in the Western Hemisphere. Any attempt to promote the liberties of democracy in Latin America fell by the wayside in favor of supporting anti-communist strong men who could ruthlessly put down communist-induced unrest and insure stability, thereby preventing the emergence of any communist government in the Western Hemisphere.

Within two weeks following Batista's 1952 coup d'état, Washington gave its recognition and support to his unconstitutional government. Following the coup, U.S. Secretary of State Dean Acheson had advised U.S. President Harry S. Truman to recognize the Batista government on the grounds that Batista had "made satisfactory public and private statements with regard to Cuban intention to fulfill its international obligations; its attitude towards private capital; and its intention to take steps to curtail international communist activities in Cuba." "We have no reason to believe that Batista will not be strongly anti-communist" Acheson rightly concluded (USDOS 1983, 871). Not only was Batista strongly anti-communist, he was also stoutly anti-democratic. After taking power by undemocratic means, which was not out of the ordinary in Cuban politics, Batista suspended constitutional guarantees, including the right to strike, and put forth a new constitution enabling him to deny the freedom of speech, press, and assembly at any time. He began censoring the media and jailing or exiling his political opponents. Political parties were no longer recognized and the Cuban legislature was replaced with a special council made up of Batista supporters (Staten 2003, 72). Yet the political stability Batista provided in Cuba was rewarded with continued U.S. economic and military support and increased private investment.

U.S. President Dwight D. Eisenhower had put the matter bluntly at a National Security Council meeting on Latin American policy in February 1955: "[F]ree government cannot work among Latins" (cited in Schoultz 2002, 418). Still, when Vice President Richard Nixon made his Caribbean and Central American tour in 1955, he stopped over in Cuba to meet with Batista and publicly congratulate him for "Cuba's continuing cooperation with . . . [the U.S.] in the defense of the principles of freedom and democracy" (cited in Ibid.). Ironically, four years later when Nixon met with Fidel Castro following the Cuban Revolution and repeatedly requested that democracy be respected and elections promptly held, Castro replied that "the people did not want elections because the elections in the past had produced bad government" (cited in Ibid., 420).

By the time Fidel Castro and his band of guerrillas began emerging out of the Sierra Maestra mountain range in late 1958, U.S. influence over the island had become immense. The U.S. sugar quota was guaranteed at an amount of more than 50% of all Cuban sugar. U.S. companies had invested over $1 billion in Cuba and owned half of all agricultural land, controlled almost 50% of Cuba's sugar productions, 90% of its utilities and tele-communications, 50% of its railroads, and had large interests in mining, oil refineries, rubber by-products, livestock, cement, and tourism. 80% of all Cuban imports came from the United States, 22% of these being foodstuffs as U.S. producers had pressured Cuba not to produce foodstuffs locally so they could have a guaranteed market in Cuba (Staten 2003, 84). The cultural and social influences of the United States had also taken deep root in Cuban society. Staten (Ibid.) suggests that the Cubans' social identification with the United States, "coupled with the realization that Americans would never view Cubans as equals, led to a growing disenchantment with and resent-ment toward the United States." Furthermore, Washington's support for Batista led Cubans to greatly question the United States' commitment to democracy. In general, Cubans had come to see that "the Americans on the island did not live up to their stated ideals and standards of fair play and equal treatment" (Ibid., 85).

These factors lay at the forefront of the anti-American shaded nation-alism purveying within the anti-Batista opposition movements in Cuba, most notably the 26th of July Movement led by Fidel Castro and the various student opposition groups linked with it. With history as an indicator, it was also clear to these groups that overthrowing the Batista regime would most likely lead to a confrontation with the U.S. (Staten 2003, 73; Domínguez 1978, 145).

2.3. Democracy Promotion via Regime Overthrow: The Cuban Revolution

Batista's dictatorship fell in the first hours of New Year's Day, 1959 as he and his cronies fled to the Dominican Republic. Seven days later, Fidel Castro and his revolutionary group entered Havana and took control of the central government. U.S.-Cuba relations would never be the same again. As the new revolutionary government began implementing its program, the relationship between the two countries started a rapid and intense downward spiral that ultimately erupted in nuclear standoff.

Washington's initial approach to the new Cuban government during its first few months was one of caution. The U.S. Government wanted to see democratic elections, but this seemed to be of second importance to that of suppressing communist influence within the revolutionary government. After meeting with Fidel Castro in Washington during April, 1959, Vice President Nixon reported to the Secretary of State that the Cuban leader was "either incredibly naïve about Communism or under Communist discipline

– my guess is the former, and . . . his ideas as to how to run a government or an economy are less developed than those of almost any world figure I have met in fifty countries." "But because he has the power to lead," Nixon concluded, "we have no choice but at least to try to orient him in the right direction" (USDOS 1991, 476). As 1959 dragged on, however, it became clear that the U.S. would be unable to orient Castro in the direction Washington had in mind. The initial land reform and tax policies of the revolutionary government greatly threatened U.S. interests and met with strong resistance from the U.S. business community. As the nationalization of U.S. property began and government displays of anti-Americanism increased, Washington became increasingly anxious. One State Department memorandum during the summer of 1959 emphasized "the apparent movement of the Cuban Government toward the left and indications of the influence of international communism." "If the Cuban revolution is successful," the memo reasoned, "other countries in Latin America and perhaps elsewhere will use it as a model." Thus, the State Department concluded that the United States must ultimately decide "whether or not we wish to have the Cuban revolution succeed" (Ibid., 604, 605).

In January 1960, the State Department reported to the National Security Council that by June of 1959 the Eisenhower Administration "had reached the decision that it was not possible to achieve our [U.S.] objectives with Castro in power." The main objective, therefore, became "to adjust all our [U.S.] actions in such a way as to accelerate the development of an opposition in Cuba which would bring about . . . a new government favorable to U.S. interests" (Ibid., 742). By October, Eisenhower had approved a program developed by the State Department and the Central Intelligence Agency (CIA) "to support elements in Cuba opposed to the Castro Government while making Castro's downfall seem to be the result of his own mistakes" (Ibid.). Thus, within the first year of the Cuban Revolution the U.S. Government had decided on the policy of regime change.

The decline in U.S.-Cuba relations accelerated as the events of 1960 began heating up. In February the first trade agreement between Cuba and the Soviet Union was signed and the Soviets extended $100 million in credit to Cuba for the purchase of industrial equipment. A month later President Eisenhower ordered the CIA to begin training Cuban exiles in Guatemala for an invasion to overthrow the Castro government. In June the Cuban Government nationalized U.S. petroleum refineries after the U.S. companies refused to process Soviet crude oil. This action was followed by the cancellation of the Cuban sugar quota by the U.S. and the Cuban Government's subsequent nationalization of all U.S. properties in Cuba. In November 1960, two weeks before U.S. presidential elections, Eisenhower issued the embargo banning the export of all U.S. products to Cuba and followed this move with the termination of diplomatic relations with Cuba (Staten 2003, 89-96).

Accompanying these events was the increasing realization, as a State Department memo of April 1960 describes, that "the only foreseeable means of alienating internal support [for the Castro government] is through disenchantment and disaffection based on economic dissatisfaction and hardship." Therefore "every possible means should be undertaken promptly," the memo concluded, "to weaken the economic life of Cuba . . ., to decrease monetary and real wages, to bring about hunger, desperation and [the] overthrow of [the] government" (USDOS 1991, 885).

With the cancellation of the Cuban sugar quota and the subsequent prohibition of U.S. exports in place, the U.S. strategy of regime change through economic coercion had begun. This was accompanied by a covert plan of action code-named Operation Mongoose, under which destabilization activities were carried out with the overriding goal of creating an internal revolt in Cuba, which would topple the Castro government. These covert operations employed activities ranging from intelligence collection and anti-Castro propaganda campaigns to sabotage operations and assassination attempts inside of Cuba (U.S. Senate, Select Committee to Study Governmental Operations with Respect to Intelligence Activities 1975, 142). In 1978 former CIA director Richard Helms described to a U.S. House congressional committee these covert destabilization programs against Cuba "that were constantly running under government aegis:"

We had task forces that were striking at Cuba constantly. We were attempting to blow up power plants, we were attempting to ruin sugar mills, we were attempting to do all kinds of things during this period. This was a matter of American Government policy. This wasn't the CIA alone (U.S. House of Representatives, Select Committee on Assassinations 1979, 125).

During April 1961, just months after taking office, U.S. President John F. Kennedy, anxious to bring about the desired internal revolt of the Cuban people and be done with Castro, ordered the invasion of Cuba by CIA-trained Cuban exiles. Having been developed under the Eisenhower Administration, the invasion plans that Kennedy inherited, as a CIA memorandum from January 1961 explains, envisaged "the seizure of a small lodgement on Cuban soil by an all-Cuban amphibious/airborne force of about 750 men," which would take place following a tactical air campaign aimed at the destruction of "all Cuban military aircraft and naval vessels constituting a threat to the invasion force." The planners at the CIA expected these operations to "precipitate a general uprising throughout Cuba and cause the revolt of large segments of the Cuban Army and Militia." "A general revolt in Cuba," it was reasoned, "if one is successfully triggered by our operations, may serve to topple the Castro regime within a period of weeks." In the case that events did not go according to plan and the expected uprising in Cuba failed to materialize, the CIA figured that "the lodgement established by our force can be used as the site for [the] establishment of a provisional government which can be recognized by the United States . . . and given overt military assistance. The way will then be paved for United States military intervention aimed at [the] pacification of Cuba, and this will result in the prompt overthrow of the Castro Government" (USDOS 1997, Doc. 9).

The invasion, known as the Bay of Pigs, commenced as scheduled at 1 a.m. on April 17. It failed miserably and most all of the approximately 1,200 invaders were quickly captured by the Cuban military. The consequences of this small invasion, however, were of much greater proportions than any military damage caused by the attack. Firstly, the attack provided Castro with an opportunity to consolidate his power and eliminate virtually all remaining opposition on the island (Staten 2003, 97). During the air bombings that took place before the landing of the U.S.-backed exile army, most of the CIA's 2,500 agents and their 20,000 suspected sympathizers were rounded up and thrown in jail. Furthermore, the U.S. had failed to hide its involvement in the operation, a factor that provided Cubans the proof that the U.S. was out to destroy the Cuban Revolution (Ibid.). This not only enabled Castro to mobilize the Cuban public against the United States, but it ultimately led to closer military relations with the Soviet Union and the fateful decision to place nuclear missiles in Cuba. After the Bay of Pigs fiasco, President Kennedy expanded the import ban to include all products from Cuba and called for a re-evaluation of all U.S. programs to overthrow the Castro government, "which fall short of outright war" (cited in U.S. Senate, Select Committee to Study Governmental Operations with Respect to Intelligence Activities 1975, 135).

The Cuban Missile Crisis came in October 1962 when a U-2 reconnaissance mission gathered photographic evidence of Soviet offensive missile sites on Cuban soil. The U.S. responded with a naval blockade of Cuba and over the course of the ensuing days the situation was able to be defused with an agreement between Kennedy and Khrushchev that the Soviet missiles would be removed from Cuba in exchange for a pledge by the U.S. that it would not invade Cuba and that it would remove U.S. missiles from Turkey. Once again, as in the Spanish-American War, the United States came to an agreement over Cuba with a foreign power while not involving Cuba in the negotiations. Castro angrily demanded that the U.S. end all subversive activities, lift the economic embargo, terminate its support of Cuban exiles attempting to overthrow the government, and return Guantánamo Bay to Cuba before he would consider the crisis over (Staten 2003, 100). The U.S. pretentiously ignored his demands. During the crisis Kennedy had reasoned "that an assurance covering invasion does not ban covert actions or an economic blockade or tie our hands completely" (USDOS 1996, 436). Thus, the covert destabilization operations would continue, with the unchanged aim of using "general sabotage and harassment as an economic weapon and as a stimulus to internal resistance," as an internal review of the program undertaken during the first months of Lyndon B. Johnson's presidency describes (USDOS 2005, 555).

The chain reaction of events during these first years of the Castro government had drastic consequences for the future of Cuba. As if history were repeating itself, just as the strong influence of the United States had served to shape the Cuban republic's first political system, the reactionary behavior of the U.S. following the Cuban Revolution can also be seen in shaping the institutions of Fidel Castro's revolutionary system. In general, it is thought that the United States' aggressive reaction to the Cuban revolution provided not only the motivation, but also the justification for an extensive centralization of political power within the hands of a small ruling elite around Fidel Castro (Ibid., 97; Domínguez 1978, 137). This centralization of political power was coupled with an expansion of the government bureaucracy, leading to extreme political, social, and economic control. Domínguez (Ibid.) identifies two ways in which the U.S. policy pushed this trend. Firstly, the willingness of the United States to take hundreds of thousands of Cuban refugees fortuitously rid the Castro government of internal political opposition and dissent, enabling the development of a more politically compliant population. Secondly, the intensity of the conflict with the U.S. required an increase in the capacity of the Cuban Government to defend itself against a powerful foreign threat. This necessitated the buildup of Cuba's military defenses and internal security apparatus. In fact, the U.S. Government's covert sabotage operations actually sought to push this trend. By "damaging economically important installations," the 1964 program review explains, the Cuban Government would be forced to "divert money, manpower and resources from economic to internal security activities" and thereby be denied "the release into normal economic activity . . . " (USDOS 2005, 555, 557). Within the economic sphere, the intensity of the conflict required the socialization of the economy in order to eliminate U.S. enterprises on the island as well as Cuban private enterprises and, thus, prevent their possible collaboration with the U.S. Government.

It seems that the expulsion of the United States from Cuba was inevitable. History had shown the pattern of U.S. dominance over Cuba's internal political affairs. While the revolutionary government might have achieved change in Cuba without a major confrontation with the United States, Domínguez (1978, 145) suggests, "it would not have amounted to a revolution." Furthermore, the expulsion of the United States from the island was ground in the events of 1898, which had been strongly anchored into the revolutionary program of the 26th of July Movement led by Fidel Castro and others fighting against the Batista dictatorship. As a means of rectifying history, the events of 1898 moved to center stage in Cuban popular discourse during the early months of 1959 (Pérez 1999, 393). The revolution was seen as the final victory in the Cuban fight for independence that had begun more than a half-century earlier. Upon the arrival of Castro and his guerillas in Havana, one Cuban journalist described the revolution as such: "The revolutionary armies of 1895 . . . have reached power, finally, free of all mediating influences. We are witness to the vindication of the triumph that the United States, through its armed intervention in 1898, cheated us of . . . We have finally liberated ourselves from the complex of a protectorate" (cited in Ibid.). The reasons for these nationalistic expressions and their underlying anti-American current did not go unnoticed within parts of the U.S. Government. In the first days of the revolution's triumph, the U.S. Consulate in Santiago de Cuba reported to Washington on the "feeling that is being whipped up" among Cubans: "I think that many Cubans have always had an inferiority complex with respect to the United States, and the feeling about the Platt Amendment is not yet dead. One frequently hears that this is the first time that Cuba has actually been free, and by its own efforts despite 'opposition' from the United States" (USDOS 1991, 373).

Whereas popular rhetoric in revolutionary Cuba was rooted in the historical events of 1898, so too did the year 1898 reappear in United States public discourse. The invocation of 1898 in the United States was used not only to explain the bafflement of Americans in understanding Cuba's grievances with the U.S., but also as a means to undermine the new Cuban Government. The U.S. press and government officials alike found it generally incomprehensible that "Castro [had] rejected friendship with the country that liberated Cuba in 1898," as one daily paper concluded (cited in Pérez 1999, 394). Thus, the concept of Cuban ingratitude was once again invoked, this time to undermine the Cuban revolutionary government and reestablish the turn of the century belief of a people 'incapacitated for self-government.' The Cuban Government, as one U.S. congressman clarified, "seized American property in a country that was conceived by America, delivered by America, nurtured by America, educated by America and made a self-governing nation by America." "When ingratitude on the part of a nation reaches the point that it has in Cuba," the congressman continued, "it is time for American wrath to display itself in no uncertain terms" (cited in Ibid., 395). Indeed, American wrath was displayed, the uncertainty of its terms resulting in quite extreme consequences.

2.4. Democracy Promotion via Economic Punishment and Isolation

As the previous section highlights, the U.S. strategy of bringing about economic destruction in Cuba through the trade embargo and covert sabotage operations, both of which aimed at inciting an internal revolution to overthrow the Cuban Government, was formulated in the first years after the Cuban Revolution. While the covert sabotage actions of the CIA tapered off during the later part of 1960s, the general strategy of economic denial and isolation remained.

The first change of a new policy direction toward Cuba came under the engagement policy of U.S. President Jimmy Carter during the late 1970s. Pursuing a policy aimed at rapprochement, Carter emphasized in a presidential directive of March 1977 that the United States "should attempt to achieve [the] normalization of . . . relations with Cuba" through "direct and confidential talks . . . with representatives of the Government of Cuba." He also directed the Attorney General to "take all necessary steps permitted by law to prevent terrorist or any illegal actions launched from within the United States against Cuba" (U.S. National Security Council 1977, 1). Carter re-established diplomatic relations with Cuba by opening the U.S. Interests Section in Havana and secret talks with the Cuban Government led to new agreements on fishing rights and maritime boundaries between the two countries. He also revoked the travel ban that had prevented U.S. citizens from traveling freely to Cuba. However, the break down of East-West détente and the growing internationalism of the Castro government, reaching its peak with the arrival of Cuban troops in Ethiopia during 1978, served to break off the talks and U.S.-Cuba relations once again froze (Staten 2003, 116).

With the arrival of anti-communist crusader Ronald Reagan in the White House in January 1981, relations between the two countries further deteriorated. Reagan saw Cuba as the menacing satellite within the orbit of the Soviet Union's "Evil Empire." It sought to destabilize the Western Hemisphere with its active support for leftist movements such as the Sandinistas in Nicaragua and the FMLN in El Salvador and these activities had to be fiercely countered. Reagan moved against the Sandinista government in Nicaragua by organizing and funding the Contras and his administration supplied massive military and economic support to the military junta in El Salvador. In Grenada, where Cubans were helping construct an international airport, which Reagan judged to be "suspiciously suitable for military aircraft, including soviet-built long-range bombers," the president sent in U.S. troops to topple the left-wing government of Bernard Coard and "restore order and democracy" (Reagan 1983).

Reagan's plans to bring democracy to Cuba took a different approach. Alongside restricting all travel by U.S. citizens to Cuba by prohibiting any expenditure of money on the island, Reagan brought about two important developments in U.S. Cuba policy. Firstly, his administration established new instruments for promoting democracy in Cuba, which were used to accompany the economic embargo, and secondly, he enabled a powerful new political force in the formulation of U.S. Cuba policy. Two years after taking office, President Reagan launched Project Democracy "to foster an infrastructure of democracy" throughout the world (Reagan 1982). Reagan's Project Democracy gave birth to the National Endowment for Democracy (NED), which today serves as the central component of the U.S. Government's democracy promotion apparatus – its mission is to "strengthen democratic institutions around the world through nongovernmental efforts" (NED 2008). The aim of establishing an organization like NED was to transform the covert propaganda activities undertaken by the CIA in the ideological battle of the Cold War into overt activities. Thus, instead of using covert methods to channel money to oppositional organizations in foreign countries to promote political change, the U.S. Government decided it wiser to create a public-private donor organization that could overtly fund foreign political opposition groups for political work. The aim was merely to provide the interventionist, foreign political activities of the U.S. Government with a more legitimate public appearance (Lowe 2008).[3]

At the same time the National Endowment for Democracy was being established, which would begin funding projects to promote a democratic transition in Cuba, the founding of another organization, the Cuban American National Foundation (CANF), was also taking place. Until the 1980s Cuban exile groups had been active in Florida, where many anti-Castro groups carried out commando style raids and terrorist actions against Cuba. However, as a large U.S. minority group, Cuban Americans had no organizational influence in Washington politics. With the founding of CANF during the Reagan Administration, the anti-Castro conservative sector of the Cuban American community was able to entrench itself in the formulation of U.S. national policy on Cuba.

Some of the very first NED grants were directed to CANF and the organization developed a close relationship with NED throughout the 1980s, receiving over $700,000 in grants for Cuban democracy promotion projects

---

[3]   NED was established by the U.S. Congress and set up as non-governmental organization, although its status is more in the likes of a quasi-governmental organization due to its dependency on the U.S. Government. NED is funded primarily through annual congressional appropriations and in turn, it is subject to congressional oversight, U.S. Government auditing and reporting rules, as well as the U.S. Freedom of Information Act, thereby blurring the lines between a private NGO and a government organization. NED serves as a sort of financial conduit by funneling its annual funds to other democracy promoting organizations in the U.S. as well as in foreign countries.

(Rohter 1992). This was, of course, in spite of the fact that NED was to fund only organizations that did not engage in partisan activities and that were expected to work outside of the United States. CANF also built up a strong political lobbying network, contributing hundreds of thousands of dollars to the election campaigns of members of Congress who were in positions to influence U.S. policy on Cuba and those who oversaw NED appropriations (Goodman 1992). Through its growing influence in Washington, CANF successfully lobbied for the establishment of Radio and TV Martí, which receive large amounts of congressional funding to broadcast anti-Castro, pro-democracy shows into Cuba. Although these broadcasts have been continuously jammed by the Cuban Government, the programs continue to receive budgets of roughly $40 million annually. By the end of the 1980s the Cuban American National Foundation had developed close relationships with the U.S. Congress, the executive branch, government agencies like the U.S. Agency for International Development (USAID), and quasi-public organizations like NED. Through this "web of relationships with the government," Haney and Vanderbush (1999, 341) suggest, the organization was able to carve out a "role as a near co-executor of policy." The group's Cuba policy coup d'état came in the 1990s with the passage of U.S. congressional legislation that anchored the U.S. embargo into United States law, thereby tying the legal removal of the embargo to the presence of a democratic government in Cuba.

2.5. A New Environment for Old Strategies

The beginning of the 1990s marked two astounding events, which greatly changed the international environment for U.S. efforts to bring down the Castro regime and democratize Cuba. Firstly, since the 1970s a wave of democratization had been spreading across the globe. Beginning in Southern Europe, it then moved to sweep up non-democratic regimes in Latin America, Africa, and Asia before ripping through the iron curtain and democratizing the eastern European Soviet Republics and transforming even Russia itself (Huntington 1991). Secondly, the collapse of the Soviet Union between the years 1989 and 1991 had extreme consequences on the Cuban economy. Basically overnight, Cuba not only lost roughly $8 billion of annual Soviet subsidies and aid, but also 80% of its foreign trade relations. Soviet petroleum exports to Cuba dropped from 13 million tons annually to roughly 2 million tons and food shipments fell by more than 50% (Staten 2003, 126). Between 1989 and 1992 the Cuban economy contracted by 50% and its GDP declined by 34.8% (Hoffmann 2001b, 4-6). During this so-called Special Period in Time of Peace, the Cuban Government was forced to institute more or less a war economy, marked by the complete rationing of all products (Ibid.).

It was at this time that the U.S. embargo began reaching full effect, compounding the rather vulnerable situation the Cuban Government found itself in. The regime was faced with finding new import sources, new export markets, and desperately needed capital in order to shop around on the international market. As a way out of the crisis, Cuba pursued a strategy to integrate itself into the global economy by promoting tourism and foreign direct investment. It pursued this route by offering joint ventures to foreign firms in industries such as tourism, mining, telecommunications, natural gas, and pharmaceuticals. It also set up several free trade zones offering manufacturers tax holidays for their investment (Staten 2003, 127, 128; Sweig 2007, 45).

In spite of the confident predictions of Western policy makers that the Castro regime was on the brink of collapse and would inevitably become the next victim of the global wave of democratization, Cuba had undergone neither regime collapse nor any process of political liberalization. The U.S. Government perceived an "inability of Cuba's economy to survive current trends," and judged this environment to provide "the United States and the international democratic community with an unprecedented opportunity to promote a peaceful transition to democracy in Cuba" (Cuban Democracy Act of 1992, §6001 (6); hereafter CDA). Several U.S. policy makers, as reflected by Deputy Assistant Secretary for Inter-American Affairs Robert Gelbard (1992), held that the "long-standing American policy of economic and political isolation of Cuba" and its "firm and clear policy on the administration and enforcement of the embargo" was the most potent tool "to bring about a peaceful democratic transition in Cuba."

During the 1990s, therefore, the United States moved to further economically strangle the Cuban Government, which meant tightening up the long-standing embargo in order to close off Cuba's escape route of developing its tourism industry and acquiring foreign investment in joint ventures. The new push came with the passage of two laws, the Cuban Democracy Act of 1992 (CDA) and the Cuban Liberty and Democratic Solidarity Act of 1996 (Libertad).[4] As both titles suggest, the laws sought to promote a democratic transition in Cuba. The strategy remained consistent with the status quo policy of engineering the economic collapse of the Cuban regime and creating internal opposition. Both laws sought to move against trade with Cuba by third countries and foreign firms through extraterritorial sanctions in the hopes of further destabilizing the Castro

---

[4]   The CDA and the Libertad acts can be found in title 22 of the United States Code, Chapters 69 and 69A. All subsequent citations of the acts in this study refer to the U.S. Code for the CDA and the congressional format for the Libertad Act, H.R. 927, listed in the references under U.S. Congress 1996.

regime during its greatest economic troubles. The acts also moved to strengthen the bottom-up approach to promoting a democratic transition in Cuba through efforts aimed at supporting civil society in Cuba – i.e. developing internal opposition against the regime. The CDA called for the allocation of U.S. governmental assistance "through appropriate non-governmental organizations, for the support of individuals and organizations to promote nonviolent democratic change in Cuba" (§6004 (g)). The Libertad Act re-emphasized this strategy by authorizing the U.S. president to furnish assistance and support to individuals and independent NGOs "to support democracy-building efforts for Cuba" (§109 (a)). Along with these measures, the acts emphasized the continuation of Radio and TV Martí as "effective vehicles for providing the people of Cuba with news and information" (Libertad, §2 (7)) and communication channels were opened up by re-establishing telephone services between the two countries and reinstating daily, direct mail delivery through the U.S. Postal Service (CDA, §6004 (e), (g)).

An important aspect of both the CDA and Libertad acts was the influential role played by the Cuban exile community. The lobbying activities of the Cuban American National Foundation, which had begun under the Reagan Administration, reached their peak with the passage of these laws (Brenner/Haney/Vanderbush 2004, 72). Furthermore, the importance of the Cuban American voting bloc in Florida greatly helped push both George H.W. Bush and Bill Clinton towards this hardened approach on Cuba (Petras/Morley 1996).[5]

As the 1990s came to an end, however, the Clinton Administration left office with no results to show for promoting democratic political change in Cuba. Also at this time, a small crack appeared in the embargo. Due to the influential lobbying activities of the U.S. agriculture industry, the U.S. Congress passed the Trade Sanctions and Export Reform Act of 2000, which allows for the export of U.S. agricultural and medical products to Cuba, provided that financing is made by third country financial institutions only

---

[5] In the case of the CDA, as the legislation was going through the U.S. Congress, the administration of U.S. President George H.W. Bush had expressed its opposition to the act. However, presidential candidate Bill Clinton had strongly endorsed the CDA during his campaign fund-raising activities in Miami and criticized the Bush Administration for missing the "big opportunity to put the hammer down on Fidel Castro and Cuba" (cited in Petras/Morely 1996, 270). In the midst of his presidential campaign for reelection, this pressure pushed Bush to sign the CDA into law – it is no coincidence he chose Miami for the official signing ceremony. The drafting of the Libertad Act of 1996 received great impetus from CANF, but there was much congressional and presidential resistance to the act. However, as the legislation was awaiting congressional action, the Cuban Air Force shot down two U.S. planes belonging to the anti-Castro group Brothers to the Rescue for having violated Cuban airspace. Consequently, the incident enabled quick passage of the Libertad Act by Congress and the legislation was subsequently singed into law by President Clinton (Brenner/Haney/Vanderbush 2004, 69; Staten 2003, 134).

and payment is made with cash in advance (§7202 (b) (1)). The act, passed by Congress during a presidential election year, drew criticism from the election campaign of Texas Governor George W. Bush, who expressed his opposition to "changing the sanctions against Cuba until Fidel Castro or the Cuban Government allow free elections, free speech and freedom for political prisoners" (Holmes/Alvarez 2000). Following his successful election to office, U.S. President Bush made clear that his administration apposed any further "attempt to weaken sanctions against the [Cuban] regime" and would take the necessary measures "to enhance and expand the enforcement" of the embargo (Bush 2001).

Two years after taking office, President Bush turned his sights toward Havana. His attention was grabbed in April 2003 when the Cuban Government moved against opposition and dissident groups on the island. Over the course of two days Cuban security forces rounded up and arrested upwards of 100 dissidents. Seventy-five were tried in Cuban courts on charges of carrying out counterrevolutionary activities in the service of the U.S. Government with the purpose of overthrowing the Cuban Government and the majority of those accused received sentences reaching up to 20 years imprisonment (Bond 2003, 118). In the wake of this crackdown on political dissent, the Bush Administration responded with a new, invigorated program to crackdown on Castro and bring about a transition to democracy in Cuba. In October the president established the Commission for Assistance to a Free Cuba and charged it with finding ways to hasten a democratic transition in Cuba and planning policies for a post-transition scenario. The commission released its first *Report to the President* in 2004, which laid out a policy framework with a new impetus to "deny revenues to the Cuban dictatorship" through the strengthening of the embargo; to "break the information blockade" of the regime and "illuminate the realities of Castro's Cuba" through a propaganda campaign; and to "empower Cuban civil society" via stepped up financial assistance (CAFC 2004, 7). Together, these actions aim "to undermine the survival strategies of the Castro regime and contribute to conditions that will help the Cuban people hasten the dictatorship's end" (Ibid.).

In response to the commission's suggestions, the Bush Administration has tightened up the embargo by further restricting U.S. travel to Cuba and reducing the amount of dollar remittances that can be sent to Cubans on the island. These actions have been accompanied by more aggressive enforcement of the embargo and punishment of U.S. citizens and firms found in violation of the embargo laws. The U.S. program to empower Cuban civil society has been increased to an amount of $45.7 million for 2008 to finance projects aimed at promoting a democratic transition in Cuba. In addition, a U.S. Cuba Transition Coordinator, Caleb McCarry, has been appointed within the Commission for Assistance to a Free Cuba to plan and support the democratization of Cuba (CAFC 2007).

Likewise, the general environment in which the new policies have taken place has also intensified. In the CAFC 2006 *Report to the President,* the chapter entitled "Hastening the End of the Castro Dictatorship" begins with a note stating: "For reasons of national security and effective implementation, some recommendations are contained in a separate classified annex" (2006a, 14). This mysterious annex continues to remain classified. It should, therefore, be of no surprise that the Cuban Government presumes these secret recommendations "are highly dangerous and constitute a less than subtle announcement of further terrorist attacks, new attempts to assassinate government leaders and even a military invasion" (Republic of Cuba, Ministry of Foreign Affairs 2008a). If history were to serve as an insight, this reading would not seem farfetched. Furthermore, the hostile public comments of two Cuban American congressional representatives who recently called for the assassination of Fidel Castro certainly must arouse suspicions of what the United States has in store with its new Cuba initiative (Cuba Source 2004; NBC6 2006). The transfer of power to Raúl Castro has not stopped the invigorated confrontation. As State Department Deputy Spokesman Tom Casey told reporters following the power transfer: "He [Raúl] is simply a continuation of the Castro regime, of the dictatorship" (Associated Press 2008a). In general, the new aggressive environment that has emerged under the Bush Administration seems to have catapulted U.S.-Cuba relations a half-century back into time. And indeed, the new U.S. offensive is ultimately a continuation of the same policies that were developed a half-century ago, only the covert sabotage operations have been substituted with overt measures to destabilize the Cuban regime by seeking to promote political dissent and government opposition in Cuba by empowering Cuban civil society.

Over a century has now passed since the United States intervened in Cuba's war for independence in 1898. All the while it has tirelessly sought to establish democracy in Cuba. While having transplanted democratic institutions under the U.S. military occupation following the defeat of Spain, the Platt Amendment independence endowed onto Cuba by the U.S. served to nullify any hope for the development of a functioning democratic process. The sovereignty of Cuba over its internal affairs was trumped by the desire of the United States to secure its interests and needs while disregarding those of ordinary Cubans. It was this environment that laid the seeds of the revolution of 1959 and kindled its nuance of anti-American sentiment. With the ascendancy of Fidel Castro's revolutionary government, the United States lost its dominant place on the island and regime change became the order of the day. Once again, the structures for political change erected by Washington helped push the country in the opposite direction of democracy.

Since the intense days of the disastrous Bay of Pigs invasion and subsequent missile crisis, the U.S. has attempted to promote a democratic transition via a policy aimed at bringing about the collapse of the regime through economic coercion and the inflammation of internal opposition.[6] Equally during this time, the Cuban Government has resisted any transition to democracy.

In an effort to explain the continuance of this U.S. policy of aggressive confrontation with Cuba, Bernell (1994) suggests that it is the long lasting result of the Cuban Revolution's successful challenge to the United States' two most sensitive policy spheres in the Western Hemisphere: the Monroe Doctrine and the containment of communism:

> It was the combination of these two affronts that provoked such a sharp, unyielding response from the United States . . . [The U.S.] has staked a great deal of time and energy in maintaining its position. To abandon it now, absent any major change in Cuba, would be to admit failure . . . The hostility has been maintained for so long it is the comfortable and familiar 'place' to be (Ibid., 98).

Likewise, Pérez (2002, 251) proposes that the "U.S. policy [has] assumed a life of its own. Its very longevity serves as the principal rationale for its continuance." Is the U.S. policy merely what some consider "a subterfuge, a convenient excuse for a hostile policy now that its original justification – the Cold War – is over [?]" (Schoultz 2002, 398). Or is it a policy that today can help bring about the goal of the United States, highlighted by President George W. Bush (2006), "to have a free, independent, and democratic Cuba as a close friend and neighbor [?]" To shed some light on this question it would be useful to examine the theoretical premises that underlie the U.S. strategy to promote a transition to democracy in Cuba. Firstly, the idea that the destruction of the Cuban economy is somehow tied to democratization and this relationship can be positively influenced by the U.S. sanctions. And secondly, the idea that Cuban civil society, existing within a closed non-democratic state, can be developed and promoted by the United States to help bring about a transition to democracy in Cuba.

---

[6]   This is not to say that other measures have not been pursued. During the 1970s, a Senate investigative committee found "concrete evidence of at least eight plots involving the CIA to assassinate Fidel Castro from 1960 to 1965." "The proposed assassination devices," the committee's report described, "ran the gamut from high-powered rifles to poison pills, poison pens, deadly bacterial powders, and other devices which strain the imagination" (U.S. Senate, Select Committee to Study Governmental Operations with Respect to Intelligence Activities 1975, 71).

3. Top-down: The Theoretical Framework

In order to better understand the impact of Washington's top-down strategy on the promotion of democratic change within Cuba, the following chapter constructs a general theoretical framework within which this structure of economic denial and isolation can be analyzed. It is generally recognized that democracy promoters have two paths available to them within the socioeconomic sphere through which they may pursue their goals. A democracy promoter can support and assist economic and social development in non-democratic states with the aim of creating domestic pressures for democratization, or conversely, they may attempt to undermine such developments as a way of engineering the collapse of a non-democratic regime and then provide assistance to its new democratic successor (Burnell 2004, 103, 104; Dauderstädt/Lerch 2005, 6). These strategies are grounded in a line of democratization theory emphasizing the importance of socioeconomic structural changes within a society that may create internal pressure for democratic change within a non-democratic state.

As already highlighted, the United States has chosen the route of undermining economic development in Cuba via its long-standing economic sanctions. The Libertad Act states clearly that "the foreign policy of the United States . . . [is] to bring democratic institutions to Cuba through the pressure of a general economic embargo" (§301 6(A)). The premise is that economic denial will bring about continued economic failure in Cuba, thereby creating popular dissatisfaction with the government while simultaneously weakening the government's ability to repress this popular dissent, leading to the destabilization of the regime and, ultimately, its collapse. This approach was highlighted in the 2006 report of the Commission for Assistance to a Free Cuba, which stresses "that the U.S. Government maintain economic pressure on the regime to limit its ability to sustain itself and repress the Cuban people" (2006a, 29). Although almost 50 years in existence, while clearly having a sustained affect of disorienting the Cuban economy, this strategy has still failed to produce regime change and further the prospect of a democratic transition. Thus, a theoretical look into the interplay between a regime's economic performance and the possibility of regime collapse and subsequent transition to democracy will serve to give a better incite into the mechanisms at work within this phenomena.

3.1. Economic Failure and Democratization

As a general rule, scholars believe that poor economic growth or economic crisis will lead to regime destabilization and increase the likelihood that a non-democratic regime will breakdown – just as incumbent leaders in democracies are more likely to be swept out of office during times of economic downturn (Huntington 1991; Linz/Stepan 1996; Przeworski/Limongi 1997; Geddes 1999; Diamond 2003). Huntington (1991) identified economic crisis as an influential factor in several democratic transitions during the 1970s and 1980s. Indeed, several existing studies testing sizeable data sets seem to support this trend. Londregan and Poole (1990) analyzed economic data from 121 countries between the years 1950 and 1982 and found that the probability of a government to be overthrown by a coup was substantially influenced by a country's rate of economic growth, or in this case, a lack thereof. The data shows regime change to be 21 times more likely to happen among the poorer countries in their sample than among the wealthier ones. A study by Przeworski and Limongi (1997) also shows a high correlation between economic failure and regime destabilization in poorer countries. The authors conclude that even democracies, "particularly poor democracies, are extremely vulnerable to bad economic performance" (Ibid., 169).

In order to explain this, scholars have identified poor economic performance, or outright economic crisis, as one of several structural factors at play between a regime's legitimacy and its performance, which, depending on a society's perception of these two dimensions, can interact in a way as to cause regime destabilization and possible regime collapse (Merkel 1999, 123). All governments rely on some degree of internal legitimacy in order to maintain power. Much like democracies, non-democratic regimes are able to mobilize legitimacy for their rule by means of several instruments, such as nationalism and ideology as well as genuine government performance. However, what non-democracies lack is the possibility of deriving legitimacy from the institutionalized procedures of democracy, which bestow a government with two robust sources of legitimacy. Not only can incumbent democratic governments – whether performing poorly or not – claim legitimacy from the elections that brought them to power, but they can also be voted out of office in the next election, a factor that legitimizes the political system itself (Huntington 1991, 50; Linz/Stepan 1996, 79). Thus, lacking these significant, inherent system-legitimizing factors, a non-democratic regime often depends on legitimizing its rule by socioeconomic performance alone, frequently with the goal of bringing about economic modernization (Merkel 1999, 125). In what Huntington (1991, 50) terms the "performance dilemma," if a regime fails to deliver its promises in the area of economic development, its legitimacy is subject to crumble.

The process of how performance failure can lead to regime destabilization seems apparent enough. Because a particular regime has based its legitimacy to rule on its performance, it will most likely bear the brunt of the blame in times of failure and may become thrust into a precarious crisis of legitimacy. Disaffection caused by failed socioeconomic performance, for example, may find resonance in large parts of society as well as within parts of the government itself, thereby triggering reactions such as the mobilization of popular opposition, uprisings against the regime, or even splits within the ruling elites. As Merkel (1999, 125) points out, a crisis of legitimacy will become particularly dangerous for a regime if massive social protest is accompanied by a split within regime elites over the question of whether to respond to the unrest with sheer state repression or by opening up a path for some sort of political liberalization.

Likewise, it is thought that the performance dilemma can also act as a boomerang, destabilizing non-democratic regimes that are perhaps even performing well (Huntington 1991; Diamond 2003; Merkel 1999). If non-democratic leaders are achieving results in the performance sector, such as successfully modernizing the economy, their regime and the costs that come with it – lack of freedoms and rights, unwarranted repression, etc. – may come to be seen by the people as unnecessary. Its legitimacy then weakened by growing opposition, the regime will face the same dilemma over how to respond to the unrest. In this view, the performance dilemma has the potential to create a no-win situation for any non-democratic government.

Linz and Stepan (1996, 79, 80) take the performance dilemma argument further by elaborating the interplay between the factors of legitimacy, the perception of alternatives existing within society, and the amount of coercion available to the regime. They emphasize that where no strong perception of alternatives to the non-democratic system exists – whether in society, regime elites, or both, – the regime, whether suffering under lower levels of legitimacy or not, will have the power to continue its rule by coercion alone. If, however, the belief in perceived alternatives grows, or if the coercive capacity of the regime declines, then the more likely that a destabilization episode may lead to regime collapse (Ibid.). Thus, not withstanding a continuous strengthening of a regime's coercive apparatus, the stronger the belief in alternatives that exist in society, and with it the growth in active opposition, the weaker the regime's coercive apparatus will become and accordingly, the less likely the regime will be able to hold power by the use of coercion alone.

Obviously, the use of repression and coercion to maintain power is not the only option available to authoritarian regimes caught in the destabilization trap. Regime elites may decide to begin liberalizing the political or economic systems, or even initiate an all-out process of democratization with the hopes of retaining leadership. In general, however, one should not presume that liberalization or repression will be the immediate response chosen by a regime to deal with growing popular opposition, but rather a range of options can be thought to be available to governments in destabilizing situations. Many options, however, may only succeed in diffusing the situation for the short term, thereby simply delaying the ultimate decision of increased repression or political liberalization.

As a structural element, economic failure alone does not cause the breakdown of non-democratic governments and a subsequent transition to democracy. While it may push a regime into a destabilizing situation, it is ultimately the actions and reactions of various actors, such as regime elites and supporters, opposition groups, and the masses, that will determine the outcome of a destabilization situation. The structural changes responsible for the destabilization of a regime will define a corridor of action, within which these various actors will attempt to implement their preferred strategies in order to achieve an outcome most favorable to their particular interests (Merkel 1999, 124). Accordingly, because different types of regimes organize elite actors and society in different ways, the preferences of actors and their degree of maneuverability will differ in accordance with different regime types. Economic failure, therefore, is thought to affect different types of non-democratic regimes in different ways (Linz/Stepan 1996; Geddes 1999). Furthermore, even If economic crisis does trigger the breakdown of a regime, it is not implied that a transition to democracy will be the ultimate outcome. As O'Donnell and Schmitter (1986, 3) emphasize, transitions are characterized by "extraordinary uncertainty," with "numerous surprises and difficult dilemmas" along the path from a non-democratic regime "toward an uncertain "something else.""

A study by Geddes (1999) highlights the importance of the varying political dynamics among non-democratic regimes, which influence the options available to the various actors during destabilization situations. These dynamics will, of course, greatly affect the probability of regime collapse and any ensuing political transition. Geddes looked at the economic trends in approximately 130 authoritarian regimes during the year prior to their collapse.[7] In regimes that fell between the years 1946 and 1993 she found a strong correlation between poor economic performance and regime collapse or overthrow, but this relationship varied with the type of non-democratic regime.[8] Military regimes were found to be the most susceptible

---

[7] Evidence of a year's gap between economic downturn and regime collapse has been found by Przeworski and Limongi (1997, 169), who discovered that the political effects of economic crises tend to occur within a year's time.

[8] Geddes (1999) grouped her data set into three types of non-democratic regimes: military, single-party, and personalist. Her classifications are determined according to the control

to collapse, whereby per capita income *grew* an average of 0.4% during the year prior to the fall. In turn, personalist regimes that collapsed in this time period experienced an average of 0.5% *decline* in per capita income. And remarkably, in states with single-party regimes that collapsed during this period, per capita income *declined* by roughly 4% on average during the year prior to the transition (Ibid., 135, 136).

To explain this trend, Geddes employed simple game theory to highlight the role of incentives and options available to regime elites and supporters during times of destabilization and possible transition. Options, of course, shape incentives, which will likewise shape actions. An actor's perceived position within a new regime following the collapse of the old was found to play a determinant role in the outcome of destabilization. Military regimes, for example, were found to be the most prone to essential internal splits within the officer corps that can exacerbate destabilizing situations and are, thus, more prone to political transitions. Poor economic performance or economic crisis, especially when accompanied by popular opposition, will more than likely hasten and exacerbate these internal divisions (Ibid., 135). The incentive in this case is that most all but the highest of regime officers can expect life after democratization with their status and careers untarnished (Ibid., 131; also see Huntington 1991, 116). Single-party regimes were found less likely to undergo internal splits in the face of economic crises. In the instance that leaders do face competition from rivals, "the benefits of cooperation are sufficiently large to insure continued support from all factions" (Geddes 1999, 131). The incentives for single-party government personnel in this case is staying in office, and most would rather wait patiently on the sidelines in times of leadership struggles than risk being on the losing side. This leads Geddes to conclude that "on average, single-party regimes have been remarkably resilient" and are less vulnerable to transitions "even in the face of long, severe economic crises" (Ibid., 139). Likewise, personalist regimes were also found to be quite resistant when faced with economic downturn or crisis. In large part, the clientelistic nature of loyalty that is characteristic of these regimes makes the development of internal splits less likely. As long as the regime has enough available resources to distribute benefits to its supporters, it is more likely to counteract the potential destabilizing affects of poor economic performance. Only when economic crisis is severe enough to affect the regime's resources to the point where the clientele support system can no

---

over access to power rather than institutional characteristics. Accordingly, in Geddes' military regime, access to power is controlled by a larger group of elites than in single-party regimes, and power access in a personalist regime is controlled by a smaller group of elites than in single-party regimes (Ibid., 123). Regimes that share system dynamics from one or more of these however, were not specifically discussed. She also excludes from her data non-democratic regimes maintained by foreign military occupation or military threat, so as to control for possible external variables.

longer be upheld, will the incentives for further clientele support decline and the regime will then become more susceptible to collapse (Ibid.).

In sum, the general available evidence regarding the relationship between economic failure and democratization seems to suggest that the destabilization and subsequent collapse of non-democratic regimes is more imminent in times of economic crisis. Yet as Geddes' work emphasizes, some regimes are more susceptible to breakdown than others. The factor of agency, particularly regarding regime elites, plays a principal role in the instigation or prevention of transitions and thereby the outcome of a desta-bilizing event. Thus, options and incentives matter, as the perceived position of regime elites within a new democratic successor regime will influence the outcome of any transition process. Likewise, the existence of perceived alternatives within a society to the failed policies of the non-democratic regime, and its closed and often repressive system, will play a role in pushing regime destabilization further during times of economic crisis. The more these perceived alternatives are organized, the more they will shape the uncertainty of the outcome.

3.2. Sanctioning Regime Collapse

At first glance, the logic of the U.S. policy of promoting economic destruction, premised on the belief that it will hasten the collapse of the Cuban regime, may not seem too implausible. Denying Cuba the resources it needs for economic development should lead to sustained economic hardships, thereby increasing popular socioeconomic dissatisfaction among Cubans. While also denying to the Cuban Government financial resources and hard currency, the regime should no longer be in a position to finance the strengthening of its coercion-apparatus in order to repress political dissent, which may eventually force a top-down opening for political change, or even outright transition – albeit even 50 years later. However, there are several drawbacks to this approach as a democracy promotion strategy.

Firstly, undermining economic development as a way of promoting democracy will more than likely have negative economic consequences on any future democratic government that may emerge. As Burnell (2004, 104) points out: "Where an economic wasteland is created so as to bring down a regime, that is a very inauspicious foundation on which to try to build a new democracy." The available evidence analyzing the relationship between economic development and democracy suggests that poor democracies stand more chance of dying than wealthier democracies. A group of scholars using data analysis from a study of 135 countries between the years 1950 and 1990 found that, "when poor countries stagnate, whatever democracies happen to spring up tend to die quickly. Poverty breeds poverty and dictatorship" (Przeworski et al. 1997, 305). Almost fifty years ago Seymour Lipset (1959, 75) proposed that "the more well-to-do a nation, the greater the chances that it will sustain democracy." Since Lipset's seminal article, several studies testing large sets of data have found evidence supporting his premise that a positive relationship between economic prosperity and democracy exists (see Londregan/Poole 1990; Przeworski/Limongi 1997; Biox/Stokes 2003). Thus, while economic failure may indeed undermine the survival of an authoritarian regime and bring about its collapse, the economic success of an authoritarian regime may be more likely to create an encouraging foundation for the survival of an incoming democratic regime (Huntington 1991, 35).

Secondly, It is not so much a country's level of wealth alone that is thought to sustain democracy, but rather the various socioeconomic by-products of industrialization and successful economic development such as urbanization, increased economic independence and security, rising education levels, and the development of a well-educated, socially organized middle-class. All these factors are thought to modernize the social sphere and facilitate the development and spread of democratic beliefs, norms and values within a society (Lipset 1959, 84). Several scholars, therefore, have emphasized the democratizing aspects of these socioeconomic changes within non-democratic states, thereby arguing that successful economic modernization will generate pressures for democratization (Huntington 1991; Diamond 2003; Biox/Strokes 2003). Accordingly, democracy promotion strategies that seek to undermine a country's economic development would also be undermining the development of these democratizing by-products.

Democracy promoters wishing to influence political change by supporting successful economic development in non-democracies have several options, such as development aid and trade liberalization attached with conditionality and political dialogue, as well as the encouragement of foreign direct investment (Dauderstädt/Lerch 2005, 7). This is not to say that such a strategy will lead to democratization, nor necessarily to the development of democracy-supporting socioeconomic by-products suggested by the modernization theory. Burnell (2005, 105), for example, warns of the negative side effects of opening up a country to the global economy, particularly when this leads to growing socioeconomic inequalities within society, which can undermine any positive perceptions of economic liberalization. Furthermore, Bueno de Mesquita and Downs (2005) have highlighted the strategies of several autocratic states, in particular China and Russia, which have found ways to enjoy the benefits of substantial economic development while simultaneously deflecting, or at least postponing, pressure for political liberalization by simply regulating the availability of the key "strategic goods" that are required by opposition groups for the development of "strategic coordination."

Thirdly, the strategy of undermining economic development to promote a transition to democracy may itself be counteracted by the very policy instrument used to achieve this goal: economic sanctions. The use of economic coercion as a policy instrument, as we shall see, is perhaps not as suited as some would like to believe for the ambitious goal of promoting democracy in non-democratic states.

Economic sanctions as a form of statecraft have been increasingly used throughout modern history. In the last several decades economic sanctions have often been imposed both unilaterally and multilaterally with the goal of bringing about the demise of authoritarian leaders. Fidel Castro is not the only autocrat to have successfully defied economic sanctions. United Nations sanctions failed to bring about the collapse of Saddam Hussein's Ba'ath regime. Kim Il Sung, in the face of long enduring sanctions, continues to hold on to power in North Korea and was not deterred from acquiring nuclear capabilities. Most recently economic sanctions have failed to strangle the military junta in Burma, which continues to survive.

A practical definition of economic sanctions agreed upon in the various literature is the deliberate withdrawal, or threat of withdrawal, of economic resources by a 'sender' country, with the aim of effecting a political change in the politics of a 'target' country[9] (Chan/Drury 2000; Hufbauer/Schott/ Elliott 1985). Galtung (1967) pointed out early on that such a definition should also not fail to rule out the mere desire of the sender country to punish the target by depriving them of some value they would have received under normal conditions. In such cases, even if the target does not comply with the demands, the sender at least enjoys the gratification of "knowing (or believing) that the sinner [the target country] gets his due, that the criminal has been punished" (379).

Much existing literature on economic sanctions has addressed the question of whether sanctions are an efficient tool in achieving foreign policy goals. The results have been mixed. In one of the most comprehensive studies on the efficacy of economic sanctions to date, Hufbauer, Schott and Elliott (1985) analyzed the outcome of 103 economic sanctions episodes between the years 1915 and 1984 and drew the conclusion that "in most cases, sanctions do not contribute very much to the achievement of foreign policy goals" (79). In accordance with their criteria for success, the authors found that in only 36% of the cases overall did economic sanctions have an impact on reaching the policy objective sought by the sender. The results ranged from having a modest impact to full achievement of the

---

[9] This definition excludes sanctions episodes resulting from regulatory trade disputes, in which market placement strategies of national firms lie at the forefront.

objective. A further study by Pape (1997), however, has found this success rate to be even lower.

In sum, the analysis carried out by Hufbauer, Schott and Elliott (1985) reveals that economic sanctions pursuing only modest changes in a target country's policies (e.g. improvement on human rights) are the most likely to be rewarded with "at least modest success" (41). In such cases, the sender is more likely to be rewarded if the target is an ally of the sender or at least neutral in the relationship between the two countries. This later factor has been corroborated more recently by Drezner (2000), who finds higher success rates in economic coercion that is directed at an allied target. Of the Hufbauer, Schott and Elliott (1985) cases in which a sender sought a more significant change in the target country's behavior (e.g. ending a military conflict), the sanctions were much less likely to succeed. Quite often these episodes were associated with the explicit or implicit aim of destabilizing target governments (Ibid., 39). In such destabilization episodes, the success of sanctions was found to be highly dependant on "companion measures" such as covert actions and quasi-military operations (Ibid., 43). However, the simple fact that these sanctions episodes were accompanied by additional covert or overt programs of destabilization, undoubtedly attests to the failure of the economic coercion itself being capable of achieving the goal sought by the sender (Pape 1997, 97).

A more recent study by Marinov (2005) looks further into the efficacy of economic sanctions in their role of destabilizing target countries, finding them to be more effective than previously thought. His data analysis shows that the chance of country leaders loosing power at any given time increases by 26% when they are subject to sanctions (565). "A leader who is subject to economic sanctions in a given year," Marinov concludes, "is, on average, more likely to lose office in the following year" (570). As previously discussed, lower economic growth hurts the political survival of regime leaders, and indeed, one of the main destabilizing consequences of sanctions found in Marinov's study is that sanctions will put pressure on a target regime by lowering economic growth. Not surprisingly, it is mainly democratic leaders who are more likely to be replaced when subject to economic sanctions, and the risk grows over time. Due to their domestic accountability, democratic leaders are much more susceptible to domestic preferences and lobbying efforts during times of sanctions than are less accountable leaders of non-democratic regimes.[10] The study also found leaders of mixed regimes[11] to have a "greater risk of removal than autocrats

---

[10]   A variable not addressed in Marinov's study however, is whether new leaders emerged in democratic targets not as a direct result of the incumbent leader being voted out of office due to the impact of the sanctions, but rather as a result of term of office limits which prohibited the incumbent leader from seeking an additional term.

[11]   Marinov (2005, fn. 20) classifies mixed regimes in accordance with the Polity IV dataset

and the effect only increases with time" (Ibid., 571). This dynamic correlates with the findings of Geddes (1999) that the more prone a regime is to leadership splits, the more prone it is to destabilization. It follows, therefore, that sanctions will have a greater impact in destabilizing those non-democratic governments that are most prone to splits within the ruling elites, highlighting the role of incentives in complying with the demands sought by the sanctions.

Even in light of the positive correlation Marinov found between economic sanctions and destabilization of country leaders, the author is unable to explain the failure of long-lasting, unsuccessful sanctioning episodes involving countries such as Cuba, Iraq, and North Korea. "Long-run sanctions against some of the world's most vicious regimes," he explains, "have done much to obscure the average effect of economic sanctions . . . [and] constitute highly atypical outliers in a set of pressure episodes which are, typically, associated with greater government instability" (Ibid., 575).

The varying findings on the impact of sanctions suggest that the efficacy of this form of statecraft is not as clear-cut as some would suggest. In fact, the degree to which an episode of economic coercion contributes to the sender's policy objective is often as ambiguous as a sender's public justification for implementing the sanctions. On the side of the sender, other variables may be at work with which the efficacy of sanctions can be judged. Chan and Drury (2000, 6), for example, point to the role of sanctions in pleasing domestic constituencies in the sender county. In this case, the sanctions are viewed not by what they are achieving in a foreign policy sense – whether the sanctions are contributing to reaching the sender's stated policy goal – but by the domestic benefits reaped by the sanctioner, often in the form of electoral rewards. As previously discussed, the anti-Castro Cuban American community, in particular the political lobbying group CANF, came to wield immense influence in U.S. Cuba policy during the 1980s and 1990s. The state of Florida is home to the majority of roughly 1.3 million Cuban Americans. It is also home to important electoral votes in U.S. presidential elections. As a result, the campaigns of presidential candidates generally arrive in Miami touting a hard-line, anti-Castro policy in exchange for the votes of Cuban Americans (Bremmer 2006; Pérez 2002; Sweig 2007). Yet, while the status quo U.S. Cuba policy is undoubtedly rewarded with important electoral votes, for the purpose of this study I will concentrate on policy rewards in the form of a change in the target country's policy, or to a lesser degree the mere political destabilization of the Cuban Government.

An important aspect of sanctions, many studies emphasize, is that the prospect for target country compliance is dependant on the perceived costs

---

as "being neither as accountable as democracies nor as free of domestic control as autocracies."

of the sanctions versus the perceived benefits of compliance (Chan/Drury 2000, 7). Plainly, if the costs of the sanctions incurred by the target government outweigh the costs of compliance, then the target will have the incentive to comply with the sender's demands. Obviously, during a sanctions episode in which the sender is seeking a regime change and political transition in the target country, as is the case with U.S. policy on Cuba, there will be little if no incentive for the target regime to concede, as this would entail its complete demise. However, Sanctions produce not only economic costs but they also create political costs for a target regime. Marinov (2005, 566), for example, premises that "for [economic] coercion to work, the political stability of the target should suffer more from coming under pressure than from conceding." A goal of the sender, therefore, is to alter the power relationships within the target state, in particular, dividing the masses from the elites in the hope that the public will increase anti-government activity while they perceive their leaders to be weakened by sanctions (Allen 2008). A recent study by Allen (Ibid., 920) suggests that "targeted publics will take action against their government when the benefits associated with such action are high and the costs are reasonably low." But because the costs of antigovernment activity are already high in most non-democratic states, and because sanctions may be used by the target government to justify raising repression even further, the "likelihood of an increase in antigovernment activity in those states," Allen (Ibid., 924) reasons, is "improbable."

At the same time, economic sanctions may ultimately produce such political, economic, and social effects in a target country that the economic coercion actually leads to political stabilization, thereby counteracting the sender's goal of political destabilization (Galtung 1967). What Galtung (Ibid., 388) designated the conventional, or "naïve" theory of economic warfare, was the belief by the sender that a proportionate relation between economic denial and political disintegration exists. In other words, the higher the target's costs inflicted by the sanctions, the higher the degree of political disintegration that will take place in the target. Indeed, this relationship has been most recently premised by the Commission for Assistance to a Free Cuba (2006a, 29), which reasoned, "the more economic pressure there is on the [Cuban] regime, the greater the likelihood there will be dramatic and successful change for the Cuban people." What Galtung saw to be lacking in this 'naïve' conception of sanctions is the recognition of the principles of adaptation and substitution.

Measures of adaptation and substitution undertaken by the target country can counter the possible political destabilizing affects of economic sanctions on two levels. Firstly, if a target's citizens adapt to the hardships created by the economic denial, it is possible that group solidarity will be increased, thereby leading to social integration rather than disintegration, which may also reinforce political integration. Thus, Galtung (1967, 389) premised that due to the psychological effects of social adaptation, the "value-deprivation may initially lead to political integration and only later – perhaps much later, or even never – to political disintegration." Secondly, because sanctions create opportunities for third parties to function as substitute trade partners, economic disintegration can be countered as the target government will seek new trading partners and reorient its economy to counteract the effects of lost trade (Ibid.; Chan/Drury 2000, 16). Chan and Drury (2000, 4) emphasize the opportunities for target countries to find substitute trading partners due to the increased economic interdependence of the world system and the greater range of alternative suppliers and markets. As a consequence, this environment "implies less trade asymmetry and more partner diversification so that it becomes more difficult for . . . [economic] coercion to succeed" (Ibid.). This last factor has led to an increasing consensus among scholars that in the absence of international sanctions, the application of unilateral sanctions will be effective only in rare cases (Haass/O'Sullivan 2000, 123).

The preceding discussion has attempted to provide a theoretical insight into the efficacy of economic sanctions in destabilizing a target regime to bring about regime change. Existing evidence suggests that economic sanctions, while perhaps not necessarily achieving their main objective, may achieve some success in regime destabilization. At the same time, one should not overestimate their capacity to destabilize, as different target regimes will prove more resilient than others. Additionally, the more time the target has to adjust, the more likely it will find substitute trading partners and reorient its economy to lessen, if not altogether counter, the economic effects of the sanctions. This will particularly be the case where sanctions are confined to unilateral implementation. With this, as Galtung (1967) has shown, economic sanctions have the potential to produce various social and psychological effects within the target country, which may lead to a regime's political stabilization rather than destabilization, thereby creating the environment that sanctions actually seek to destroy.

While there exists a positive correlation between poor economic performance and regime destabilization, the utilization of economic sanctions as a tool to promote this phenomenon may ultimately backfire on the democracy promoter by producing political effects within the target country that may counter the variables at play between poor economic performance and regime destabilization. Economic sanctions may enable a regime to deflect blame arising from socioeconomic disaffection away from its performance legitimacy by holding the sanctions accountable for the poor economic performance. Moreover the sanctions may enable a target government to mobilize nationalism and anger against the sanctioning country, whereby the regime may gain a second flank in the area of performance legitimacy:

Standing against an outside aggressor. Lastly, as a democracy promoting strategy, economic sanctions may be unfit to bring about such a major political change as the costs of compliance are great. After all, democratization involves a complete reorientation of institutional structures and power resources, which require elite actors of non-democratic regimes to have incentives and society to have strong perceived alternatives to the present system. The more sanctions can create such an environment in the target country, the more success they may have.

With this chapter I have attempted to demonstrate the logic of economic starting points for democracy promoters, particularly the utility, or disutility, of implementing economic sanctions as a way to create pressures for democratization through economic dissatisfaction and hardship. While the United States pursues the economic development path of democracy promotion in non-democratic, communist states such as China and Vietnam by engaging these governments and societies through development aid, trade, and direct foreign investment, the Cuba policy chosen by the U.S. aims at economic denial to promote the collapse of authoritarianism and a democratic transition. History has shown that this strategy has failed to bring about the democratization of Cuba. An empirical analysis of the U.S. embargo, therefore, should help give an insight into the possible reasons underlying this failure.

4. Top-down: The Empirical Analysis

Since its inception, the basic goal of the U.S. embargo has been to destabilize and weaken the Cuban Government through economic coercion and political isolation, thereby undermining its economic performance, inducing popular disaffection, and creating antigovernment activity to bring down the regime, at which point a new, democratic regime can be installed. So why has this not happened during the last half-century? In order to gain a better insight into the reasons behind the failure of this top-down approach to promote a democratic transition in Cuba, the following chapter presents a detailed analysis of the U.S. embargo policy along with its consequences within the economic, political, and social realms in Cuba. Following on the analysis laid out in the previous chapter, the emphasis is placed on the following aspects: The degree to which the embargo is creating economic pressure on the Cuban regime; shaping perceptions of alternatives to the present regime among government officials and ordinary Cubans; creating positive incentives for movement toward democratic political change; and finally, whether or not these factors are delegitimizing and destabilizing the Cuban Government.

4.1. Economic Effects: Malfunctioning Unilateralism

In the first few years after President Eisenhower banned all U.S. exports to Cuba, the Cuban economy underwent tremendous disorientation, most notably because Cuba had relied on the U.S. for 80% of its imports (Staten 2003, 84). When Kennedy took away all remaining sectors of the U.S. market from Cuban exports, the sanctions hit still harder. Between 1959 and 1963 U.S. exports to Cuba fell from $438.5 million to roughly $63 million and Cuban imports to the U.S. dropped from $474.6 million to a mere $55,000 (Schreiber 1973, 395). Durable consumer goods basically disappeared from the shelves of Cuban department stores, causing the Cuban Government to instigate the complete rationing of basic hygienic items, clothing, and food. These shortages were further exacerbated by the ensuing breakdowns on production lines and paralysis of certain infrastructures, due mainly to the lack of spare parts for the U.S. made machinery. This displacement greatly affected transportation, oil refineries, and sugar mills, thereby taking its toll on food distribution and, naturally, the sugar harvest, Cuba's export lifeline (Ibid., 396, 397).

These initial hardships created by the economic coercion, however, actually served to counter the U.S. strategy of regime change and work against the long-term interests of the United States in several ways. Firstly, the initial economic disruption mainly affected middle-class Cuban retailers and manufacturers, who, with no products to sell, found it increasingly difficult to stay in business. As the U.S. Government had planned, this was the social group most aligned with the United States and also the most likely to withdraw their support from the Castro government. However, withdrawing their support translated not into antigovernment activity, but rather emigration to the United States, thereby relieving the revolutionary government of some pressure created by the sanctions and, most importantly, internal dissent and oppositional political pressure (Pérez 2002, 247, 248). The Cuban Adjustment Act of 1966 further contributed to this trend by effectively granting political asylum to all Cubans who reached the United States. Thus, the U.S. was ultimately providing relief to Cubans from the very hardships it had created through its plan to incite popular mobilization against the Castro regime (Ibid., 249). "The logic of the [U.S.] policy," as Pérez (Ibid.) candidly highlights, "required containing Cuban discontent *inside* Cuba." For many Cubans, crossing the Florida Straight to escape the economic hardship was easier, and most likely safer, than the alternative of engaging in open political opposition in Cuba. Secondly, the sanctions naturally pushed the Cuban Government to find substitute trade partners, thereby driving Cuba into the waiting arms of the Soviets. This consequence, of course, served to ultimately undermine the U.S. policy of Soviet containment (Schreiber 1973, 404).

Indeed, the willingness of the Soviets to step into the economic void created by the U.S. embargo greatly helped relieve pressure from the sanctions. The resulting Cuban-Soviet trade agreement of 1960 arranged for the Soviets to take the majority of the Cuban sugar harvest in return for six million barrels of oil annually and the remaining 20% to be paid in convertible currency, which enabled Cuba to shop for some trade in the Western market. By 1961 the Soviet bloc took 75% of Cuban exports and supplied 86% of Cuba's imports (Ibid., 391). Thus, while the initial effects of the U.S. embargo may have hit the Cuban economy hard, Cuba's quick reorientation of its trade toward the communist bloc greatly enabled the island to dampen, if not almost counter, the U.S. embargo throughout the rest of the Cold War.

Following the collapse of the Soviet Union, and thereby Cuba's subsequent loss of the majority of its trade relations, the situation of course changed. At this point, the already decades-old embargo began reaching its full effect. As the Cuban Government undertook its strategy of integration into the global economy, it began attracting foreign investment from several European and Latin American countries, Canada, and China in industries such as tourism, mining, telecommunications, oil, and pharmaceuticals (Sweig 2007, 45). It was this trend that the U.S. sought to prevent by extending the economic sanctions internationally in order to back the Cuban Government into a corner. The first move came with the Cuban Democracy Act of 1992 (CDA), which sought to impose the U.S. embargo extraterritorially by subjecting foreign subsidiaries of U.S. firms engaged in trade with Cuba to the same principles of U.S. jurisdiction as their U.S. national counterparts. This move was accompanied by intimidation and direct threats toward third countries, particularly those of the former Soviet trading bloc that continued to provide assistance to Cuba. The CDA enabled the U.S. Government to sanction these countries by terminating their eligibility for U.S. foreign aid and disqualifying them from the forgiveness or reduction of any debt owed to the United States (§6003 (b)). Both of these strategies were broadened and strengthened with the Cuban Liberty and Democratic Solidarity Act of 1996 (Libertad).

The Libertad Act involved numerous strategies to extend the U.S. economic sanctions into the international arena. One strategy was to pursue this route within the United Nations Security Council. Under the U.S. assertion that "the acts of the Castro government, including its massive, systematic, and extraordinary violations of human rights, are a threat to international peace" (§101 (1)), the United States hoped to use Article 39 of the U.N. Charter to bring about international sanctions on Cuba. Needless to say, this attempt clearly failed. Beginning in 1992, the same year the CDA was passed, and now for the past 16 years, the UN General Assembly has voted annually in an overwhelming majority in favor of condemning the unilateral embargo. A recent vote in October 2007 consisted of 184 votes in favor of lifting the sanctions, against a mere four votes in opposition: the United States, Israel, Palau and the Marshall Islands (Parsons 2007).

Thus, failing to convince the international community to adapt the United States' hard-line approach to promoting democratic political change in Cuba via an international embargo, the Libertad Act was also armed with threats and intimidation in attempt to widen the embargo. Title I of the act emphasizes the continued use of the U.S. vote within international financial institutions against the admission of Cuba into these institutions, or the granting of any loan to the Cuban Government by these institutions. If for some reason Cuba is granted a loan by such an institution, in spite of U.S. opposition, then the U.S. will retaliate by withholding the equal amount in payments to the responsible institution (§104, §105). Like the CDA, title I of the Libertad Act threatens third countries directly by allowing for the reduction of U.S. financial assistance, to any country, in an amount equal to the amount these countries continue to assist or support Cuba, including any non-market based trade, the continued use of the Lourdes military base in Cuba (§106), or the continued involvement in the construction of the Juraguá nuclear facility in Cuba (§111).

The most radical tools with which the Libertad Act sought to widen the U.S. embargo internationally were developed in titles III and IV of the law. These sections sought to hinder the joint venture strategy of the Cuban Government by going after third parties involved in expropriated U.S. properties in Cuba. Title III of the act allows U.S. nationals with outstanding property claims in Cuba to sue foreign firms that are involved in any business undertaking with the Cuban Government that involves these expropriated properties. Such firms are held liable in U.S. courts "for money damages in an amount equal to . . . the amount certified to the claimant by the [U.S. Government] . . . plus interest; or the fair market value of that property . . . [at] either the current value . . . or the value . . . when confiscated plus interest, whichever is greater; and court costs and reasonable attorneys' fees" (§302). Likewise title IV of the act sought to further hinder any foreign companies or individuals from doing business with the Cuban Government by denying U.S. entry visas to any foreign nationals caught 'trafficking' in U.S. expropriated property. This includes any foreign individual, whether a corporate executive or a shareholder with a controlling interest in an entity, as well as their families (§401).

Following the passage of the Libertad Act, numerous governments, whose citizens would be the principle targets of Libertad's titles III and IV, immediately denounced the legislation and challenged its compatibility with international law. When both Canada and the European Union threatened to bring the case to the World Trade Organization (WTO) and fight the U.S. law on legal grounds, a compromise between the parties was reached. Most likely anticipating such a reaction, the U.S. Congress had inserted a presidential waiver into the Libertad Act allowing the U.S. president to suspend title III for a period of six months at a time. Accordingly, the U.S. Government pledged to continue suspension of title III and apply ample discretion in any case involving the possible use of title IV against European firms. In exchange, the European Union agreed not pursue a dispute in the WTO, promised to place more scrutiny on any investments in Cuba by European firms which might involve expropriated U.S. property, and in addition, strengthen their efforts to promote democracy in Cuba (Smis/Van der Borght 1999, 233; Gratius 2001, 206).[12]

---

[12]   The international blowback caused by titles III and IV of Libertad consisted of claims challenging the extraterritorial effect of the law, mainly its imposition of secondary boycotts, its violation of the principle of sovereignty and non-intervention in the domestic matters of foreign states, and its violation of various rules recognized by international economic organizations such as the WTO (Smis/Van der Borght 1999, 227). Preeg (1997) has argued that the attempt to justify extraterritorial sanctions against citizens of foreign countries on foreign policy grounds, not only contradicts the principles underlying the

Whatever its international legality may be, title III of the Libertad Act has yet to be implemented. The presidential waiver allowing for the suspension of this section of the law has been invoked continuously by both Presidents Bill Clinton and George W. Bush, the most recent renewal of the suspension having been applied on February 1, 2008 (Bush 2008). Thus, the full effect of Libertad's title III has never borne fruit. The desire of the United States to extend the sanctions internationally continues to meet with unsuccessful attempts. The coercive policies of the U.S. during the 1990s did not lead to the collapse of the Castro regime, but rather Cuba was able to survive the worst of its economic crisis and by the second half of the 1990s the Cuban economy began to recover. Today, the U.S. continues to go it alone in promoting a democratic transition in Cuba through a policy of unilateral economic coercion.

The U.S. embargo, properly known as the Cuban Assets Control Regulations, was first issued in July 1963 under the Trading With the Enemy Act. The degree and reach of the regulations have been relaxed and strengthened at various times since. As it stands today, the embargo affects all U.S. citizens, permanent residents, organizations and businesses, as well as international branches and subsidiaries of such organizations and businesses throughout the world. Any violation of these regulations will result in penalties ranging from a prison sentence of up to 10 years, $1 million in corporate fines, $250,000 in individual fines, and the possibility of up to $55,000 in civil fines (U.S. Department of Treasury, Office of Foreign Assets Control 2004a, 1; hereafter U.S. Treasury, OFAC).

Apart from the exportation of food and agricultural commodities as well as medicine and medical supplies under the Trade Sanctions Reform and Export Enhancement Act, the exportation by any U.S. national of products, technology, or services to Cuba or any Cuban national, wherever they may be located, is prohibited. Likewise, the regulations forbid the purchase of any property "in which Cuba or a Cuban national has an interest" by any persons or firms subject to U.S. jurisdiction located in third countries. Thus, neither may a U.S. citizen "purchase Cuban cigars in Mexico" nor a U.S. overseas subsidiary enter into contractual relations with a foreign firm "if the contract terms include Cuba-related provisions (even if those provisions are contingent upon the lifting of the embargo)" (Ibid., 2). Strict shipping regulations prevent foreign vessels from loading or unloading freight in the United States for a period of 180 days after they have docked at a port of place in Cuba to engage in trade. Customs agents can seize Cuban goods brought into the U.S. by individual travelers at their discretion. Cuban

---

WTO multi-lateral trading system, but also violates specific U.S. commitments to it. In contrast, other spectators have seen title III of Libertad to be consistent with international law. "The United States not only commands the moral high ground on this issue," states one observer, "it also has the better of the legal argument" (Clagett 1996: 434).

assets, both government and private, are subject to freezes by the U.S. Government, including the inheritance of estates or life insurance dividends by any Cuban national. Furthermore, U.S. citizens are subject to rigorous federal regulations controlling travel and the sending of money and gifts to the island (Ibid.).

Clearly the embargo has an effect on the Cuban economy, particularly to the extent that it limits the possibility of joint ventures with firms from the advanced capitalist nations and, moreover, the Cuban Government's ability to shop freely in the global market due to its lack of hard currency (Bertelsmann Stiftung 2007, 18). In 2007, the Cuban Government reported that the U.S. embargo has cost the country more than $89 billion in economic losses to date. Cuban Foreign Minister Pérez Roque reported to the U.N. General Assembly that the embargo caused $3 billion in economic loses for Cuba in the year 2006 alone. Still, Cuba enjoyed a GDP of roughly $40 billion for 2006 (Weissert 2007).

While the U.S. embargo creates an extremely difficult economic situation in Cuba, the island is able to find relief from much of the economic pressure in several ways. Firstly, the lack of international support for the embargo has made it possible for Cuba to continuously find substitute trading partners and adapt to new and changing circumstances, helping fill the void created by the end of the massive Soviet subsidies and aid. Cuba enjoys trade with several Western capitalist states, foremost Canada, Spain, and the Netherlands, Cuba's three largest Western trading partners. Most recently, the country has developed close trade relations with Venezuela and China, which together now make up more than 50% off all trade for Cuba (Mesa/Lago 2007, 10). As Cuba's largest trading partners, the various trade agreements, investments, and generous credit lines extended to Cuba by these two countries have done much to keep the Cuban economy intact and help bolster economic growth – reported at an exceptional rate of 9.5% for the year 2007 (Bertelsmann Stiftung 2007, 16). Both countries serve as Cuba's main source of imports and provide large markets for Cuba's exports. In particular, Venezuela under the government of Hugo Chávez has emerged as Cuba's key trading partner. The close cooperation between the two countries allows for subsidized Venezuelan oil to Cuba while also providing a large export market for Cuba's surplus of highly trained medical and educational labor force. In fact, the export of medical and educational services to many developing countries has become a major foreign currency earner for the Cuban Government (Ibid., 13).

A second factor, which helps relieve pressure from the embargo, is the inconsistency of the U.S. policy itself, by allowing for agriculture trade in accordance with the Trade Sanctions Reform and Export Enhancement Act. While the law stipulates that Cuba must provide cash payments in advance, it has not hindered a modest growth in U.S. agriculture exports to Cuba.

Cuban officials report the amount of these agriculture purchases to have reached roughly $500 million annually (McKinley 2007). Other sources, however, put this figure at only slightly over $400 million (U.S.-Cuba Trade and Economic Council 2008, 2). In any case, these purchases have the minor effect of lowering overall costs of food importation due to the close vicinity of the two countries, which translates into lower transportation costs paid by the Cuban purchaser.

Thirdly, Cuban emigration to the United States serves the function of a "safety valve," helping to relieve economic and political pressures created by the embargo (Hoffmann/Whitehead 2006, 18). Under the migration accords negotiated during the Clinton Administration, the United States takes 20,000 Cuban emigrants annually. This number is even larger due to the United States' "wet foot-dry foot" policy, whereby any Cuban who reaches the U.S. is granted asylum and those who are picked up in the waters are sent back to Cuba (U.S. Congressional Research Service 2005, 31; hereafter USCRS). Thus, while the U.S. sanctions ultimately seek to raise the specter of antigovernment activity on the island, many Cubans, encouraged by the U.S. immigration policy, choose to express their economic disaffection by voting with their feet, not their voice.

4.2. Social Effects: Washington's Iron Curtain

4.2.1. Tightening the Noose

Because the U.S. Government seeks to hinder all activities of U.S. citizens which may potentially provide hard currency to the Cuban Government, the U.S. embargo, aside from its far-reaching economic prohibitions, stretches into the most intimate, personal lives of Americans. Under the Bush Administration's push to promote democracy in Cuba, the embargo regulations have been tightened in many different areas and the enforcement of violations has been ratcheted up extremely. Most notably, these efforts have been aimed at curtailing the Cuban Government's two greatest sources of hard currency: foreign tourism and remittances from Cuban exiles to the island. Consequently, the new measures have greatly diminished social engagement between Americans and Cubans, effectively isolating Cubans further from outside influences.

In its 2004 report, the Commission for Assistance to a Free Cuba estimated U.S. remittances to the island to be in the sum of $400 to $800 million annually, a portion of which, CAFC presumed, the Cuban Government "quickly captures" through transfer fees charged to U.S. remittance companies and through the resulting purchases made by Cubans at state run dollar stores (CAFC 2004, 34). Likewise, the commission estimated that the Cuban Government earns revenues of $36.2 million annually from the delivery fees of gift parcels from U.S. citizens (Ibid., 36). Thus, following the recommendations of the CAFC report, the Bush Administration established stricter regulations for gift packages and remittances to the island. Gift parcels have been restricted to a value not to exceed $200 and only one package per month may be sent to the same recipient (U.S. Treasury, OFAC 2004a, 2). Remittances to the island have been restricted from an amount of $3,000 (USCRS 2006, 6) to a limit of $300 in every three-month period per household, provided that no member of the household is a Cuban government official or member of the Cuban Communist Party (U.S. Treasury, OFAC 2004a, 4). While CAFC recognizes that both gifts and remittances "provide a critical humanitarian benefit to the Cuban people," it insists that they "decrease the pressure on the [Cuban] government to provide the basic needs of its people, enabling it to dedicate more resources to strengthening its repressive apparatus, while taking the political credit for the resultant improvements . . . in the well-being of the Cuban people" (CAFC 2004, 35).

In order to undermine the regime's hard currency lifeline of tourism, the Bush Administration has also clamped down on travel to the island by U.S. citizens. CAFC (2004, 37) reported that roughly 125,000 family visits to Cuba in 2003 had resulted in roughly $96 million in hard currency earnings for the Cuban Government. Thus, measures were undertaken to further restrict travel for family visits, educational purposes, religious purposes, cultural events, and athletic competitions. The categories of fully-hosted travel and secondary school educational exchanges were eliminated altogether.[13]

Travel by Cuban Americans for family visits has been restricted to visiting only immediate family members for a maximum duration of no more than 14 days every three-year period. In addition, travel allowances have been limited to $50 per day for the purchase of general necessities in Cuba and an additional $50 per day for transportation related expenses within Cuba (U.S. Treasury, OFAC 2004a, 2). Travel to Cuba by religious organizations and humanitarian groups was tightened after CAFC found that these licenses were being abused by persons seeking to outmaneuver the restrictions in other categories of travel. In accordance, the administration now limits the travel of larger religious organizations to only four times per

---

[13] The category of "fully-hosted travel" refers to travel to or from Cuba, whereby all costs are paid for by a third-country foreign national, a Cuban national, or the Cuban government. The reason for banning this category of travel, OFAC explains, is that persons who claimed fully-hosted travel "routinely engaged in prohibited money transactions (e.g. payment of entry and exit or docking fees) . . . [and are] also dealing in property in which Cuba or a Cuban national has an interest" (U.S. Treasury, OFAC 2004b).

year, in groups no larger than 25 persons (USCRS 2006, 14). Educational and academic travel has also been greatly restricted. The new regulations authorize educational exchanges only for undergraduate and graduate university programs, thereby excluding any secondary school exchanges. Accordingly, these exchanges must be part of a student's structured degree program, they must last a minimum of 10 weeks, and they must qualify for full credit towards the student's degree. Likewise, any professor wishing to participate in exchange programs with Cuban universities must be employed by a licensed U.S. graduate or undergraduate institution and the exchange is required to last at least 10 weeks (U.S. Treasury, OFAC 2004a, 3).

The new regulations on educational and cultural exchanges between the United States and Cuba have lead to what Martínez (2006, 38) describes as a "freezing, if not the outright abandonment, of some of the most prestigious research programs on Cuba." Before the new restrictions on travel took place in 2004, Cuba was the fourteenth most popular study abroad desti-nation for U.S. students (Lutjens 2006, 70). Following the new restrictions many programs both in the U.S. and in Cuba were forced to close down, greatly reducing the number of student exchanges. Out of nine programs for U.S. students running at the University of Havana, only three remained at the beginning of the 2004 academic year (Martínez 2006, 39). By this same time, the number of licenses issued for academic travel to Cuba had fallen from 181 to 69 (Lutjens 2006, 71). Not only has travel to Cuba by U.S. citizens to participate in exchanges declined, but likewise, travel to the U.S. by Cuban scholars, scientists, musicians, and artists has also been reduced. Prior to 2004, an average of 25 University of Havana professors per month had traveled to U.S. institutions to teach classes, speak at conferences, or conduct research. During the first ten months of 2004, however, only five professors were granted U.S. entry visas (Martínez 2006, 39). In 2004 the U.S. State Department denied 65 visas to Cuban intellectuals and scholars scheduled to participate in a congress hosted by the Latin American Studies Association in Las Vegas. Two years later, the congress, held this time in Puerto Rico, was also lacking the participation of 54 Cubans, who had again been denied U.S. visas (Lutjens 2006, 68). Cultural exchanges between the two countries have also suffered from the administration's clampdown on travel. In the period between October 2003 and February 2004 alone, over 150 visa requests by Cuban musicians and artists to participate in culture events in the U.S. were denied by the U.S. Government (Ibid.).[14]

---

[14] A strategy utilized by the Bush Administration that greatly affects the ability of Cubans to participate in academic and cultural events held in the U.S. is the revival of Presidential Proclamation 5377, first issued by Ronald Reagan in 1985. The decree enables the U.S. president to impose visa bans on persons the Secretary of State deems "officers or em-ployees of the Government of Cuba or the Communist Party of Cuba" (cited in Marino 2006, 16). Because the decree classifies any Cuban national receiving a state salary as a representative of the Cuban Government, employees of Cuban universities and scientific

These new restrictions have been accompanied by a strengthening of the embargo's enforcement. In October 2003, the president instructed the Department of Homeland Security to increase inspections of travelers and shipments between the U.S. and Cuba. This action was followed by a presidential order in 2004 directing the Department of Homeland Security to expand its policing of the waters between Florida and Cuba in order to stop pleasure boating traffic (USCRS 2006, 4, 5). Again in 2004, U.S. law enforcement authorities were directed to carry out "sting operations" against "mule networks" and other persons who illegally carry money to Cuba (CAFC 2004, 40). Accordingly, the U.S. Department of Treasury set up a Cuban Assets Targeting Group to facilitate intelligence sharing between state law enforcement agencies. This new group aims to disrupt illegal remittance forwarding networks and close "off other channels through which the Cubans are seeking to acquire hard currency" by creating targeting lists of "Cuban front companies" (Ibid. 2006b). There has been an aggressive crackdown on illegal travelers to Cuba, the licenses of several travel service providers in Florida have been suspended, and the assets of several foreign firms caught in violation of the embargo have been frozen (USCRS 2006, 2, 14).

Naturally, these stepped-up enforcement activities have required the mobilization of increased resources within the responsible agencies. Following a report released by the U.S. Treasury it was brought to the public's attention that the Office of Foreign Assets and Control (OFAC) was employing six times more personnel to enforce the Cuban embargo than the number of agents tracking the finances of Osama bin Laden and Saddam Hussein (San Martin 2004). In the time OFAC had opened 93 investigations and collected $9,425 in fines relating to terrorism-financing violations, it had worked 10,683 cases on the Cuban embargo and collected more than $8 million in fines (Ibid.). Indeed, bringing civil processes against embargo violators seems to be rather profitable. Recent enforcement information published on OFAC's website highlights the lucrative business of the embargo's strict enforcement. Spirit Airlines, Inc. was penalized $100,000 for transferring funds to Cuba in violation of its license. United Radio Inc. paid a fine of $67,574 for the actions of its Canadian subsidiary, which had shipped radios to Cuba. The selling of airline tickets to Cuba to a U.S. citizen cost a travel agency, Journey Corp. Travel Management, $1,875 in penalties. OFAC also sees it as worthwhile to expend time and resources to punish individuals seeking to enjoy world-renowned Cuban cigars. Several U.S. citizens caught purchasing Cuban cigars over the Internet were penalized with fines reaching upward of $5,000 for their crime of dealing

institutes undoubtedly fall into this category and have been subject to visa denials by the U.S. Government on a number of occasions.

"in property in which Cuba or a Cuban national has an interest" (U.S. Treasury, OFAC 2008a; 2008b).

In a 2004 speech to leaders of the Cuban American community in Miami, Secretary of the Treasury John W. Snow explained how these fanatical enforcement activities are promoting democracy in Cuba: "We are tightening the economic noose around the regime . . . At the same time, we're reaching out to the freedom-hungry people of Cuba" (U.S. Treasury, Office of Public Affairs 2004). How the punishment of U.S. citizens seeking to travel to the island or send remittances to their family members helps to reach out to 'freedom-hungry' Cubans, Mr. Snow could not exactly elaborate. He did, however, report the recent successes of 264 new embargo violation cases the office had opened, three having been referred for criminal investigation; the blocking of 10 travel companies; the denial of travel to roughly 300 people; and the repeal of travel licenses from two organizations engaged in humanitarian and religious activities in Cuba (Ibid.).

4.2.2. Engaging in Isolation

President Bush has declared that the new restrictions on remittances, gift packages, and travel, paired with the increased enforcement activity, "will prevent the [Cuban] regime from exploiting hard currency of tourists and remittances to Cubans to prop up their repressive regime" (cited in USCRS 2006, 10). The Commission for Assistance to a Free Cuba (2006, 29) reported in 2006 that the new "limitations on travel, parcel deliveries, and remittances have sharply curtailed the regime's manipulation of and profiteering from U.S. humanitarian policies." While providing no specific dollar amount of losses to the Cuban Government resulting from the new restrictions, the report states merely that the new "measures have been successful and should continue to be implemented" (Ibid.).

However, by equating the drop in U.S. travelers, remittances, and gifts reaching the island, with the decline in revenues to the Cuban Government – and thus, declaring a success in promoting democracy in Cuba – one overlooks several consequences of these actions which work against the agenda of promoting democratic political change. Most notably, the wide reaching grasp of the U.S. embargo, by outlawing tourist travel and obstructing academic, cultural, and religious exchanges between the two countries, has the effect of further isolating Cubans from the outside world. Ironically, President Bush himself has pointed out the positive aspects of promoting trade and exchange with non-democratic countries: "Trade creates the habits of freedom, which begin to create the expectations of democracy and demands for better democratic institutions. Societies that are open to commerce across their borders are more open to democracy within their borders.

And for those of us who . . . believe in . . . universal values that promote human dignity, trade is a good way to do that" (cited in Griswold 2002).

Like President Bush explains, opening up closed societies to the globalized world may encourage and cultivate changes in beliefs and world views within these societies, which help facilitate the growth in popular perceived alternatives to the undemocratic regime and the lack of political rights the society is subject to (Diamond 2003, 22). Paradoxically, the policy makers behind CAFC recognize that the Government of Cuba has wide-reaching control over "newspapers, radio, and television," a factor that extremely hinders the "full access to independent information," and enables "the government to maintain its continued survival" (2006a, 21). Thus, part of the strategy suggested by the commission is to "break the regime's information blockade" in order to "illuminate the realities of Castro's Cuba" and provide Cubans with "reliable information on events in Cuba and on alternatives to the failed policies of the Castro Regime" (Ibid.). Indeed, it does not take much to presume that by building a wall between the peoples of the United States and Cuba by restricting trade, travel, and exchanges, the Cuban Government's "information blockade" will only be strengthened.

Academic and cultural exchanges between the two countries should be of high value to any democracy promoting strategy, because they can significantly encourage alternative perceptions. Not only do such exchanges serve as a type of cultural or "academic diplomacy" between the two countries, but more importantly they enable a broader and more objective knowledge of Cuban reality than that portrayed by the U.S. Government, which could very well help reduce the prolonged conflict between the two countries (Martínez 2006, 30). Social engagements of U.S. citizens in Cuba, in particular younger U.S. Americans, whether cultural, educational, athletic, or even tourism, would do much to undermine and counter the anti-American rhetoric lauded by the Cuban Government, thereby deriving it of a source of legitimacy (Haass/O'Sullivan 2000, 127). As Lutjens (2006, 75) points out, while indeed ironic, "but hardly surprising," one of the CAFC's recommendations for a post-transition, democratic Cuba is to open up and facilitate academic exchanges between the U.S. and Cuba. Washington's Cuba policy makers, however, obsessed with 'denying revenues to the Castro regime,' view the curtailment of such exchanges as a better way to promote democracy in Cuba because many "travelers and academic institutions regularly abuse this [educational exchange] license category and engage in a form of disguised tourism" (CAFC 2004, 30).

In a 2006 *Miami Herald* op-ed piece, Miriam Leiva of Ladies In White, a Cuban human rights group working in Cuba to promote human rights and democratic change, criticized the new Bush strategy of further isolating Cuba, noting the benefits that a policy of social engagement would bring:

What better way to help our current endeavor than to enable contact between the peoples. Millions of U.S. tourists could bring their ideas and both our peoples would better know each other. American students, professionals and scientists would help develop advances that are unknown here and describe the fair wages received for one's labor elsewhere. Cuban Americans would have an opportunity to exchange experiences and financially help relatives and friends who lack the most basic necessities (cited in U.S. House of Representatives, Committee on International Relations 2006, 7).

Consequently, by blocking the creation of social, cultural, and economic channels which would encourage new perceptions and understandings between Cubans and U.S. Americans, the U.S. policy of isolating the island contributes to the stability of the Cuban regime. Bremmer (2006) emphasizes a relationship between a non-democratic state's stability and its lack of openness to influences of the outside world. Non-democratic states that are isolated from global influences, he suggests, "are stable precisely because they are closed" (Ibid., 4). As previously discussed, the more perceived alternatives exist within a society, and the more organized these are, the more susceptible a non-democratic government will be to a loss of legitimacy, and thereby, an important source of its stability. The stability of non-democratic states, therefore, may be reinforced by measures that isolate the state's citizens from alternative influences (Ibid., 17). One such measure employed by the Cuban Government is its wide-reaching control over informational resources, which is exactly why CAFC strategy sees it as dire to "break the information blockade" of the Cuban Government. The U.S. embargo, however, by contributing to this blockade, ultimately reinforces the stability that the Cuban Government already enjoys through its active regulation of information resources.

Lastly, one does not need to point out the hypocritical nature of the U.S. Government in debunking the Cuban regime for quelling the rights of Cuban citizens, while at the same time impinging on the liberties of United States citizens by preventing them the freedom to travel where they please. In a letter to Secretary of State Dean Rusk, U.S. Attorney General Robert Kennedy once argued the need to end the travel embargo, emphasizing that permitting U.S. citizens to travel to Cuba would be "more consistent with our views of a free society and would contrast with such things as the Berlin Wall and Communist controls on such travel" (Kennedy 1963). Needless to say, the State Department overruled the Attorney General's proposal to lift the travel restrictions. A half-century later, the U.S. Government's undemocratic travel prohibitions on U.S. citizens, and its efforts in denying certain Cubans U.S. entry visas, continue to undermine the same open and free, democratic system it is trying to promote in Cuba.

4.3. Political Effects: Cultivating Cohesion

4.3.1. Alternatives and Incentives

As previously discussed, during a sanctions episode a target country is thought to comply with the foreign policy demands of the sender if the benefits of compliance outweigh the economic and political costs of the sanctions. In this light, the benefits of compliance serve as incentives for the target government to adopt the policy change sought by the sender. However, "to the extent that these demands impinge on the target country's core societal values, national images, or regime agenda," Chan and Drury (2000, 11) remind us, "compliance may mean more disutility to [the target] than resistance." Thus, the sender's demands play an unavoidable role in shaping the perception of alternatives within a target country's government and citizenry, and will thereby provide incentives or disincentives for change. In this same light, we have seen in chapter 3 that the factors of perceived alternatives and incentives within regime elites and citizens play a strong role in the event of political transitions, which may move, or for that matter push, actors toward democratization. The U.S. sanctions on Cuba are no different. The U.S. policy consists of numerous compliance criteria that Cuba would have to comply with in order to end the U.S. embargo and normalize relations with Washington. These criteria, of course, construct the framework, within which a perceived alternative to the present regime can be formulated among Cubans at all levels, and likewise, incentives or disincentives for political change can be generated.

Title II of the Libertad Act was designed "to encourage the holding of free and fair democratic elections in Cuba" and "provide a policy framework for United States support to the Cuban people in response to the formation of a transition government or a democratically elected government in Cuba" (§3 (4), (5)). As its central piece, title II of the act offers the lifting of the embargo and the normalization of relations in return for a democratic government in Cuba, which the United States will fully assist and support. This incentive for Cuba to democratize, however, is tied to numerous political, economic, and legal prerequisites and conditions, which will determine and guide the U.S. policy towards a Cuban transition government and thereafter any democratically elected Cuban government. Much like the wording in the United States' 1898 declaration of war against Spain to help Cubans to independence, the Libertad Act states that "the policy of the United States is . . . to recognize that the self-determination of the Cuban people is a sovereign and national right of the citizens of Cuba which must be exercised free of interference by the government of any other country" (§201 (2)). However, the conditions laid out in Libertad are designed in such a way that significantly impedes this "sovereign and national right" by allowing for extreme U.S. intervention.

According to the conditions outlined in title II (§205) of the Libertad Act, a "transition government" in Cuba will be recognized by the United States when:

[It] has legalized all political activity . . .; released all political prisoners and allowed for investigations of Cuban prisons . . .; has dissolved the present Department of State Security in the Cuban Ministry of the Interior, including the Committees for the Defense of the Revolution and the Rapid Response Brigades . . .; has made public commitments to organizing free and fair elections for a new government . . . [which are] to be held within a period not to exceed 18 months after the transition government assumes power . . ., [include the] participation of multiple independent political parties that have full access to the media on an equal basis . . ., [and are to be] conducted under the supervision of internationally recognized observers.

[It] has ceased any interference with Radio Marti or Television Marti broadcasts . . .; makes public commitments to and is making demonstrable progress in ... establishing an independent judiciary . . .; respecting internationally recognized human rights and basic freedoms as set forth in the Universal Declaration of Human Rights . . .; [and] allowing the establishment of independent trade unions . . . and . . . social, economic and political associations.

[It] does not include Fidel Castro or Raul Castro; [and] has given adequate assurances that it will allow the speedy and efficient distribution of assistance to the Cuban people.

Only with the fulfillment of the above conditions for a "transition government" will the United States then "be prepared to provide the Cuban people and transitional government with humanitarian, developmental, and other economic assistance" in order "to facilitate a peaceful transition to representative democracy and a market economy in Cuba" (§201 (4), (6)). As Hoffmann (2001a, 173) notes, from the perspective of any reform-oriented Cuban Government official, this catalog of conditions describe more so the characteristics of a non-sovereign government following a comprehensive regime change than a "transition government" moving toward reform, a factor which may actually strengthen the rigidness of the Cuban system in the short term.

Furthermore, any steps toward the full elimination of the economic embargo against Cuba can be lawfully set in motion only after the establishment of a "democratically elected government" in Cuba has received U.S. presidential and congressional approval regarding its democratic quality, to which a further catalog of far-reaching political and economic preconditions apply. In addition to the successful fulfillment of the conditions listed above, a democratically elected government in Cuba must be "substantially moving toward a market-oriented economic system based on the right to own and enjoy property . . . [and have] made demonstrable progress in returning to United States citizens . . . property taken by the

Cuban Government from such citizens and entities on or after January 1, 1959, or providing full compensation for such property in accordance with international law standards and practice" (§206 (3), (6)).

Thus, the political, economic, and fiscal polices of any post-Castro Cuban government which may come to power through free and fair democratic elections will be subject to an environment of U.S. Government perceptions regarding the degree to which these policies are meeting the lawful criteria set out in Libertad. Such an environment, of course, leaves Washington with a large degree of leverage and influence over the course of events in a post-transition, democratic Cuba (Hoffmann 2001a, 172, 173). Not only does this aspect further dampen incentives for any reform minded officials, but it also lies in direct conflict with the simultaneous U.S. recognition of the "self-determination of the Cuban people" and their "sovereign and national right" to establish a government "free of interference by the government of any other country" (§201 (2)).

Indeed, this duplicity has not gone unnoticed, neither within parts of the Cuban exile community nor Cubans on the island. One moderate Cuban American leader commented during a U.S. Senate hearing on the Libertad Act that the law, having already decided all pertinent "criteria for democracy in Cuba which only the Cuban people can have the right to determine," would transfer Cuba "from the dictatorship of Fidel Castro into the tutelage of the U.S. Congress" (cited in Hoffmann 2001b, 11, 12). Ladies in White activist Miriam Leiva has also faulted the U.S. Government for presuming what a Cuban transition must be before it can receive U.S. recognition or assistance. "Only we Cubans of our own volition can decide issues of such singular importance," she stresses, "Cubans on the island have sufficient intellectual ability to tackle a difficult peaceful transition and reconcile with other Cubans here and abroad" (cited in U.S. House of Representatives, Committee on International Relations 2006, 9). In a way rather reminiscent of the Platt Amendment, the criteria of the Libertad Act are so constructed as to lay a rather undemocratic foundation for any future, democratically elected government in Cuba.

If the stringent preconditions determined in Libertad are not enough to dampen any incentives within the various echelons of the Cuban Government for an embargo-free Cuba, then other aspects of the U.S. democracy promotion policy most definitely serve to tip the balance. The Commission for Assistance to a Free Cuba (2004, 27) emphasizes a strategy of creating "uncertainty regarding the political and legal future of those in leadership positions" as a means of "stripping away layers of support within the [Cuban] regime." One such strategy is creating a "list of henchmen" consisting of Cubans at all levels of the government "engaged in or misus[ing] their position to perpetrate human rights abuses," who will be "duly noted and appropriately sanctioned by the U.S. Government" (Ibid.).

Moreover, the recent events of the U.S. democratization mission in Iraq have surely not gone unnoticed by members of the Cuban Communist Party and government officials. In particular, the U.S. policy of de-Ba'athification in Iraq has most certainly served to heighten any fears and uncertainties among Cuban officials concerning their future place in any U.S. supported democratization of Cuba (Sweig 2007, 52). Like membership in Iraq's Ba'ath Party under Saddam Hussein, professional advancement in Cuba is best achieved by membership in the Cuban Communist Party. The party hosts roughly one million members and an additional half-million in the Union of Communist Youth, reaching into all sectors of society. It includes not only those who are true believers in the Cuban Revolution, but also the numerous, harmless opportunists who are merely seeking to advance their personal goals (Ibid.).

Several studies of Cuban political cohesion have pointed to the lack of soft-liners existing within the regime (see in particular Hawkins 2001). In fact, neither Libertad's stringent criteria for a democratically elected government in Cuba nor the discriminatory measures of the U.S. policy against Cuban Government employees seem to offer incentives for the development of reform-minded soft-liners. Both approaches serve to flame the uncertainty among Cubans in leadership positions and members of the party like the U.S. Government seeks. Yet rather than "stripping away layers of support within the regime," as the CAFC report suggests, the measures most likely serve to further consolidate and harden regime leadership while hindering the development of any soft-liners within the regime (Hoffmann 2001a, 173).

The U.S. criteria for a democratically elected government in Cuba also serve to influence perceived alternatives and incentives for change among ordinary Cubans. As with government officials and regime elites, the uncertainty created by the U.S. policy may serve more to create negatively perceived alternatives among society rather than positive incentives. Of particular importance in this respect is the issue of outstanding U.S. property claims, which Washington has placed so much emphasis on as a precondition for any normalization of relations between a future, democratic Cuban government and the United States. The Libertad Act clearly states: "It is the sense of the Congress that the satisfactory resolution of property claims by a Cuban government recognized by the United States remains an essential condition for the full resumption of economic and diplomatic relations between the United States and Cuba" (§207 (d)). The property issue is greatly complicated by Libertad's protection of Cuban American claimants who did not have U.S. citizenship at the time their properties were confiscated by the Cuban Government. The Commission for Assistance to a Free Cuba has also most recently reiterated the importance of settling property claims in a manner that shall make "no distinction . . . as to whether Cuban nationals left or stayed in Cuba during the Castro regime" (2004, 226). Thus, as Hoffmann (2001b, 12) points out, U.S. policy has ultimately transformed an internal Cuban conflict into an international conflict, in which the Cuban Government stands not in opposition to its citizens, but to U.S. citizens.

The issue of property claims is wide reaching, involving both physical and liquid corporate capital, trademarks and patents, as well as individual private property such as homes and buildings. According to an estimate by the U.S. Federal Claims Settlement Commission, the property claims of U.S. nationals, including interest, amount to roughly $6 billion (Creighton University School of Law and Department of Political Science 2007, 108; hereafter Creighton University). In addition, the claims of the Cuban exile community are estimated to be as much as $50 billion (CAFC 2004, 229). Residential property, in particular, is a highly charged political question. The Cuban Government has been warning Cubans for years that the end of the revolution and the return of U.S. nationals and Cuban exiles would result in mass evictions, thereby raising anxiety and fear among the island's population (Hawkins 2001, 453). Most recently, the Cuban Government responded to the 2006 CAFC report by warning its citizens that "if the plan elaborated by the US . . . were implemented, thousands, even millions of Cubans on the island would be confronted with the immediate cancellation of their home ownership rights." "Disregarding the laws approved after 1959," the article continues, "the occupation regime would validate claims not only by U.S. citizens, but also by the former Cuban landlords, who became U.S. nationals after leaving their country" (Prensa Latina 2007).

CAFC (2006a, 68) emphasizes the additional fact that "a democratic Cuban government will also have to address the disposition of confiscated industrial, commercial, and agricultural properties . . . [and] these decisions will be part of the process of privatization as part of a transition to an open, market-based economy." The democratization of Cuba and subsequent settlement of property claims within a process of privatization, therefore, greatly calls into question the future of the Cuban state's social programs, which significantly control rent and food prices, extend free education and medical care to all citizens, and guarantee state retirement pensions. As Sweig (2007, 44) points out, the revolution's social programs have truly provided for the social welfare of the Cuban poor and remain the envy of much of the developing world. Most Cubans have come to expect the state to guarantee these social benefits. The U.S. emphasis on economic measures of denationalization and privatization in a future democratic Cuba (see CAFC 2004, Ch. 4.) does much to spread anxiety among Cubans regarding the fate of these social entitlement programs following the end of the socialist state. The Cuban Government, in turn, plays its part in exacerbating these doubts among Cubans. As an article in the Cuban state newspaper

Granma most recently describes: "All aspects of the economy would be completely privatized including education and health services; all [agriculture] cooperatives would be dissolved and the old latifundia restored; social security and assistance would be eliminated, including all pensions and retirement plans . . .; the guidelines of the crudest neoliberalism would be rigorously applied" (Alarcón 2006).

The issue of property claims is further agitated by the fact that the United States has failed to adequately address the fate of legitimate Cuban claims against the United States. Since 1963 the Cuban Assets Control Regulations have severely restricted Cuban nationals in recovering property such as bank accounts and life insurance policy proceeds that have been frozen by the U.S. Government (Creighton University 2007, 164). In 2005 the U.S. Treasury reported $268.3 million in blocked assets of the Cuban Government and individual Cuban nationals (U.S. Treasury, OFAC 2005, 14). The Cuban Government, on the other hand, asserts that Cubans have over $100 billion in claims against the U.S. resulting from the embargo. In May 1999, after hearing evidence for thirteen days, a Cuban court awarded claims against the U.S. Government for human losses and hardships due to the embargo in the amount of $181.1 billion. The U.S. Government, of course, has not responded to these claims (Creighton University 2007, 5).

The adamant emphasis placed on property claims in the U.S. policy may ultimately prove to have counterproductive consequences by spreading fears throughout the island concerning the unpredictability of the future after a transition (Hoffmann 2001a, 175). Cubans may perceive that a transition to a U.S. supported, democratic Cuba would mean the return of the exile community to flood the country with property claims and private investment, leading to mass evictions, the emergence of a new political-economic elite, and the reassertion of U.S. dominance (Hawkins 2001, 453, 454). Thus, in the case of Cuba, it is not only a question of Cubans developing perceived alternatives to the present, undemocratic revolutionary government, but also their coming to terms with the prepackaged alternative of the U.S. designed democracy which will be implemented once a transition takes place. "As long as a transition to democracy in Cuba threatens to come in accordance with a rigidly written U.S. law," Hoffmann (2001b, 12) suggests, "it is for no one in Cuba's political leadership (or anyone even in a leading position anywhere in the state, economy, or society) an attractive or even remotely practicable appearing perspective." The historical significance of the Platt Amendment should not be overlooked. Just as it served to promote extreme involvement by the U.S. in the internal affairs of the Cuban republic, so too would the Libertad Act serve to dictate a framework of limited choices to any future democratic government in Cuba which sought to mend relations with Washington.

4.3.2. Government Legitimacy and System Blame

While Washington focuses on the "tyranny" taking place in the "tropical gulag" of Cuba (Bush 2007) in the form of human rights abuses and economic and political alienation, which undoubtedly deprive the Cuban regime of legitimacy, it refuses neither to acknowledge nor address the existing sources of legitimacy that the regime does benefit from. For one, the revolutionary government's social entitlement programs in the areas of health, education, retirement, subsidized food, transportation, and housing have greatly served the Cuban poor and do much to provide the government with an important source of legitimacy (Sweig 2007, 44; Hawkins 2001, 453). In fact, many of the revolution's social programs have been recognized internationally. Life expectancy and infant mortality in Cuba is at levels of Western, industrialized democracies (United Nations Development Programme 2007, 261). Literacy rates are also at the level of Western countries (Ibid., 269) and international standardized tests show Cuban school children greatly outscoring their counterparts in all other Latin American countries (Bertelsmann Stiftung 2007, 11). Most recently, the new alliance with Venezuela has enabled the Cuban Government to further increase public expenditures for its social entitlement programs, highlighting the government's emphasis on these structures (Ibid.).

By far, the greatest source of legitimacy for the Cuban Government is derived from the embargo and hard-line U.S. policy itself (Hoffmann/ Whitehead 2006; Sweig 2007; Hawkins 2001). The U.S. policy offers a source of legitimacy to the Cuban regime in two ways. Firstly, the embargo serves to partly deflect system blame arising from the poor economic conditions the Cuban regime helps to create. It is generally understood that the embargo is not solely responsible for the economic difficulties in Cuba, but rather many point to the unsound economic policies of the Cuban Government itself as being partly responsible (Sweig 2007; Griswold 2002; Bond 2003). The existence of the embargo, however, enables the Cuban regime to continuously blame the U.S. as the cause of Cuba's economic problems. Secondly, Washington's aggressive policy creates a source of legitimacy for the Cuban Government by allowing it to rally the population against an outside enemy (Hawkins 2001, 448). Cuban revolutionary ideology is grounded in the historical factor of U.S. hegemony over pre-revolutionary Cuba: from depriving Cubans of their independence in 1898, meddling in the country's political affairs under the Platt Amendment and supporting Batista's repressive dictatorship, to punishing Cubans for the last half-century for supporting the revolution. The U.S. historical factor underscores the revolution's ideological emphasis on the role of Cuban unity in defending the island from this outside threat (Sweig 2007, 44). Hoffmann and Whitehead (2006, 8) suggest that the Cuban regime "has

made resistance to foreign domination its central claim to . . . legitimacy."
As long as Washington continues to play the role of the menacing enemy
seeking to destroy the revolution, the Cuban Government is not subject to
economic performance legitimacy alone, but is able to enjoy this second
source of performance legitimacy it would not otherwise have – fending off
and defying the imperialist aggressor. This phenomenon is particularly highlighted by the festive celebrations in Cuba that accompany the U.N. General
Assembly's annual condemnation of the U.S. embargo. Every year Cubans
across the island tune in to the live televised U.N. debate and follow the
voting (CBS News 2004). As the Cuban Government has noted, Cuban's are
"accustomed to celebrating a crushing blow to the US blockade in the
United Nations for 14 years" now (Cuba versus Blockade 2006).

4.4. Goliath Feeds David

The above analysis of the U.S. top-down approach to democracy promotion
in Cuba highlights several factors at work within the economic, social, and
political levels in Cuba, which help explain the embargo's ineptness in
achieving its stated goal. As a consequence of these factors, the top-down
strategy serves more to counteract, rather than promote, moves toward
democratization in Cuba.

Firstly, while the embargo does hurt Cuba economically, significantly
hindering the degree of economic development the Cuban state would
clearly like to achieve, it has failed to create the economic misery that
would incite massive revolt against the regime as the U.S has long hoped
for. This is due to several reasons. In the absence of international sanctions
the Cuban Government has proven itself capable of adapting to changing
economic situations and negotiating new trade partners to fill the void
created by the collapse of the Soviet Union. The U.S. law allowing for the
export of agriculture products to Cuba has itself further weakened the
United States' unilateral measures aimed at strangling the Cuban economy.
Furthermore, the U.S. Cuba immigration policy serves to deflate both economic and political pressures that weigh on the Cuban Government by
allowing Cubans an escape from the poor economic situation the embargo
helps create.

Secondly, the restrictions on U.S. tourist travel, educational exchanges,
and religious work serve to keep the island further isolated from alternative,
international influences and ideas. Moreover, this policy also helps bolster
the stability of the Cuban Government by reinforcing the regime's strategy
of regulating Cubans' access to information. It should also be noted – and
this ties in with the next factor – that even if the U.S. were to move towards

a policy of allowing full engagement and exchange between peoples, its success may very well be hampered by those structures existing within the top-down approach that encourage reactionary defense, rather than positive behavioral change on the side of Cubans.

Therefore, thirdly, the adamant push to export a U.S. defined and U.S. guided democratic transition in Cuba serves more to spread negative anxiety and doubt among Cubans concerning a future democratization than to encourage positive alternatives to the revolution and provide incentives for democratic political change. Consequently, this aspect of the U.S. policy has the short-term effect of internally toughening and stabilizing the regime (Hoffmann 2001b, 13). More than just falling short of promoting democratic prospects among political leaders and ordinary Cubans, the U.S. policy serves to empower the Cuban Government. The regime in Havana merely has to point to the harsh policies of Washington to legitimize its rule and promote a nationalist environment against the hostile U.S. enemy. This factor enables the Cuban Government to deflect system blame arising from poor economic performance, and provides it with an extra source of performance legitimacy derived from fending off imperial aggression.

5. Bottom-up: The Theoretical Framework

In 2003, Assistant Secretary of State for Western Hemisphere Affairs Roger F. Noriega was asked by the U.S. Senate Committee on Foreign Relations how the U.S. embargo on Cuba helps promote a democratic transition in Cuba. He replied that the embargo "supports the development of civil society in Cuba by denying the regime the hard currency it needs to perpetuate itself and strengthen its repressive apparatus" (U.S. Senate, Committee on Foreign Relations 2003, 73). Noriega's statement offers important incites into the U.S. bottom-up strategy to promote a democratic transition in Cuba. By indirectly implying that government repression hinders the development of Cuban civil society, and thereby democratization, the statement begs several questions. Firstly, can civil society unilaterally democratize a non-democratic state? Secondly, what does the U.S. consider Cuban civil society to consist of, and which groups does it seek to promote in Cuba? Noriega also recognizes that the whole of the U.S. policy is tied together; that the embargo has direct consequences on the strategy to support civil society in Cuba. Thus, a third question is whether the embargo does in fact support the development of civil society in Cuba, or may it have counter-consequences? These questions will be addressed in the following two chapters.

5.1. Civil Society and Democratization

Following the numerous transitions to democracy during the last decades of the twentieth century, democratization and political development literature increasingly began turning to the concept of civil society and its importance in regards to democratization. The mass mobilization of civil society in many of these transitions was thought to have provided crucial pressure on authoritarian regimes to liberalize their political systems and democratize. This phenomenon was not confined to a particular set of societies and cultures, but was evident in many diverse countries spanning several continents. In Eastern Europe, groups like the Solidarnosc in Poland and the Charter 77 movement in Czechoslovakia were able to establish a sphere outside the influence of the authoritarian state where antigovernment opposition could be organized and mobilized. These activities presented strong alternatives to the authoritarian system, further delegitimizing the regime and contributing to its demise and subsequent democratization. The acquiescence of authoritarian regimes to political liberalization in several Asian countries, most notably South Korea and the Philippines, were accompanied by massive social mobilization which state repression alone could no longer control. The coalescence of civil society groups in Latin American countries drove the "popular surges," which helped push many authoritarian regimes into a process of democratization (Wiktorowicz 2000, 45). And finally, many transitions on the African continent were characterized by widespread civil society activity.

The composition of civic opposition in these transitions ranged from students and intellectuals, to trade unions and producer organizations, community and development groups, as well as religious, human rights, and women's groups. As Diamond (1994, 4) commented in the aftermath of this movement of global democratization, "no phenomenon . . . more vividly captured the imagination of democratic scholars, observers, and activists alike than 'civil society.'" Likewise, the concept of civil society also captured the minds of Western development organizations and democracy promoters, who increasingly began to focus on developing and assisting civil society movements and NGOs as key agents of development and democratization (Mercer 2002, 6).

Burnell (2004, 110) has warned that "the appeal of civil society as a route into democratization looks almost too good to be true." As his observation suggests, foreign assistance to civil society groups as an ultimate strategy for democratization is much more convoluted than democracy promoters often tend to view it. In fact, the concept of civil society itself is characterized by an ambiguous and contested definition. In particular, its organic composition as well as its position in relationship to the state, the personal-private sphere, and the market, are habitually quite fluid, taking different forms within different contexts. Civil society is generally seen as a collection of associational forms that exist between the individual-private sphere and the state. It consists of numerous formal and informal organizations and interest groups, including trade unions, producer organizations, community groups, religious groups, and social movements such as democracy groups, human rights groups, community groups, women's groups, etc. It is a politically characterized sphere, but situated outside the sphere of political parties, and enjoys some degree of autonomy from the state. It serves to empower collective actors orientated towards the public good by providing them with a vehicle for the articulation of interests and preferences to the state (Birle 2000, 234; Wiktorowicz 2000, 43).

Within the enduring Western, liberal tradition of civil society, spanning the works of thinkers such as John Locke, Charles de Montesquieu, and Alexis de Tocqueville, several general functions of civil society can be determined within the framework of democratization. Among the most important of these functions, by occupying a social sphere outside of the state, civil society can serve as a bulwark against arbitrary state intervention into the private sphere by monitoring state actions and holding the state accountable to these actions. Free, collective associations existing within this civil sphere are thought to serve as Tocquevillian "schools of democracy," through which civil virtues such as tolerance, trust, compromise, and civic participation can be generated throughout society. These organizations are thought to serve as collection points for "social capital," enabling citizens the possibility of greater collective action, while also serving as recruiting grounds for political elites (Croissant/Lauth/Merkel 2000, 11-14; Merkel/Lauth 1998, 4-7).

During democratization processes, civil society is thought to exercise these various functions at various times during the political transition. In general, the main functions of civil society in its relationship to democratization are twofold: to bring about democracy where it is absent and help sustain it where it exists (Diamond 1994). In its function of bringing about democracy, civil society is thought to serve as a motor for democratization by providing an organizational and informational space outside the institutions of the non-democratic state, in which perceived alternatives and preferences to the existing regime can be generated and organized into collective, anti-regime opposition (Diamond 1994, 7; Merkel/Lauth 1998, 8). Thus, civil society is seen to function not only as a counterweight to the non-democratic state, but also as a force seeking to overturn it. Characteristic of this function, Mansfeldová and Szabó (2000, 91) highlight civil society's capacity to voice and demonstrate demands for political liberalization through the organization of "spontaneous" and "direct" opposition against the regime. In this view, civil society is characterized by an anti-system agenda (Friedman 2004, 6) and emphasis is placed on carving out a sphere outside of state control, in which groups can strategically maneuver and organize opposition against the existing regime, pushing ultimately for its demise and a transition to democracy (Merkel/Lauth 1998, 9).

The second function of civil society regarding its relationship to democratization is its role in supporting and deepening democracy after a democratic transition has taken place. No longer acting as the antithesis of the illegitimate, non-democratic state, civil society is now conceived of as acting in a manner that compliments the democratic state. While continuing to serve in its capacity of restricting state power, civil society also serves to legitimize this state power (Diamond 1994, 5). Thus, once it is formally established within the framework of democracy and the rule of law, civil society checks the use of arbitrary state power into the private sphere, while also providing opportunities for greater citizen participation and communication, through which various societal preferences and interests can be articulated to the state level (Ibid., 8, 9). However, several scholars see this operational phase as the point where the collective nature of civil society activity, which may have taken place under the non-democratic regime, will decline. Mansfeldová and Szabó (2000, 91) point out that during the institutionalization of democracy, the coherence of civil society as an anti-regime opposition movement will decline actors form new organizations within the sphere of civil society, while others, due to the new "political opportunity structures," move into the political system. Schmitter (1997, 242) emphasizes that individuals and social organizations will pursue more private, special interests during this phase of the political transition and the rise of political parties and powerful interests associations will find more resonance within the democratic system than single-issue movements.

Thus, democratization literature seems to be talking about two different types of civil society. The one conceives civil society as the antithesis of the non-democratic state, characterized by its broad collective nature, its autonomous work outside the state, and its aim of delegitimizing and, ultimately, bringing about the collapse of the state. The other conceives civil society as a complimentary, legitimizing component of the democratic state, working within a lawful framework provided by the state, and characterized by more splintered collective interest group activity. This discrepancy underlines Merkel and Lauth's (1998, 12) observation that a precise classification and function of civil society in its relationship to democratization is dependent upon the various, unique context in which it exists.

While heading this warning of avoiding precise classifications of civil society in absence of its empirical context, several general suppositions concerning the democratizing potential of civil society can be drawn from the extensive assortment of existing empirical studies. Firstly, the function of civil society as a motor of democratization should not be overestimated. Schmitter (1997, 242), for example, holds that civil society, irrelevant of its strength, is not "a prerequisite either for the demise of autocracy or for the transition to democracy, nor is it ordinarily sufficient to bring about such a change in regime." Rather, transitions to democracy may be accompanied by a "resurrection of civil society," but this phenomenon will most likely occur during the end-phase of an authoritarian regime, after elite political conflict has taken place and a transition is already underway (O'Donnell/ Schmitter 1987, 48). Secondly, civil society should not be understood as an intrinsically unbiased and altruistic collective body and caution should be taken before perceiving civil society as a democracy-promoting sphere in general (Birle 2000, 236). There is always the possibility that civil society may be harnessed by undemocratic social forces and movements within a society, giving rise to an "un-civil society," which may aim at undermining or destroying democratic structures and practices (Croissant/Lauth/Merkel 2000, 26; Wiktorowicz 2000, 46). This last aspect highlights a third relevant point concerning civil society's democratizing power. As O'Donnell and Schmitter (1987, 54) suggest, even if a "popular upsurge" of unified groups supporting democratization emerges at some point during a transition, this will be "by no means a constant." Rather, its emergence, its intensity and duration, and, particularly its impact on a transition will be unpredictable.

In sum, transitions to democracy that have been characterized by the mass mobilization of anti-regime opposition and mass demands for political liberalization, particularly such cases as Poland, South Korea, and the "color revolutions" of this century, suggest that civil society may fulfill an important function of acting as a motor for democratization. At the same time, however, these developments are far from ensured. Civil society acts alongside other processes in bringing about and sustaining democracy. It "cannot unilaterally bring about democracy," Schmitter (1997, 240) posits, "[n]or can it alone sustain democratic institutions and practices once they are in place."

5.2. Harnessing Civil Society from the Outside

Democracy promoters wishing to assist the development of civil society in foreign countries can enter from below, working with groups directly on the actor level, or they can enter from above, working with host governments within the state structural level (Dauderstädt/Lerch 2005, 9). On the structural level, democracy promoters may focus on promoting institutional reforms geared towards developing state structures based on the rule of law, thereby helping to carve out a political sphere where civic organizations can legally develop and have room to maneuver. This of course entails that the democracy promoter work alongside state institutions with the aim of changing the behavior of the non-democratic government towards its society. In this case, the consent of the ruling elite for these types of assistance is of dire importance and is likely to be rejected by any non-democratic government seeking to remain in power. In fact, young, consolidating democracies may also justifiably resist such overt foreign intervention.

The other opportunity, of course, is for democracy promoters to enter from below and concentrate on assisting civil society groups on the actor level by directly conferring material and financial support to these groups and movements (Ibid.). Assisting civil society in this way in non-democratic states can be problematic, particularly where the aim of the foreign donor is to pressure for democratization by promoting and assisting opposition to the existing government. To begin with, the activities of Western democracy promoters seeking to mobilize civil society groups as an agent for democratization may meet with great resistance from the side of the host government. Particularly in non-democratic states with closed political systems, civic groups with an agenda that aims opposition against the state will most likely be limited and greatly exposed. Foreign assistance to such groups will also likely raise the suspicions of the host government, which may create counterproductive effects for these groups by making them more vulnerable to state punishment or being discredited by the state as tools of foreign political interests (Diamond 1995, Ch. 3; Burnell 2004, 110).

Moreover, if democracy promoters do have access to civil society groups, they face the problem of identifying and choosing which groups to assist (Burnell 2004, 110). One problem of immediate difficulty, Whitehead (1986, 9) points out, is wading through the often opaque "rival political groupings" in the host country, which "may go to considerable lengths to win international acceptance of their 'democratic' credentials, including disguising and misrepresenting their antecedents and even their intentions." Coupled with this problem, and perhaps even more pressing in the long run, is the degree to which the state has institutionalized society within non-democratic structures. The greater the degree of institutionalization, of course, the more likely the host government will be able to harness and control the civic groups that the donor seeks to promote. In this sense, Wiktorowicz (2000, 46) emphasizes the internal "political context that shapes and limits [civil society's] potential as an engine of political change." In recent years, several authoritarian states have undertaken deliberate strategies of self-survival by proactively liberalizing civil society activity in ways that can deflect pressures for political liberalization. By strategically entrenching civil society organizations within a "web of bureaucratic practices and legal codes," Wiktorowicz (Ibid.) suggests, the state is in a position to monitor and regulate the collective activities of these movements. This strategy not only reduces the possibility of civil society building a weighty, oppositional challenge to the state, but it also transforms civil society institutions into "more an instrument of state social control than a mechanism of collective empowerment" (Ibid., 43).

In fact, this trend seems have been a direct response to, and conse-quence of, the interventionist nature of foreign assistance to oppositional civil society groups within non-democratic states and illiberal or struggling democracies, in which the ultimate aim of the assistance is to tear down the incumbent governments in these states. Democracy promoters have begun to speak of a "backlash against" democracy promotion, and even an outright "assault on democracy assistance" (NED 2006; Gershman/Allen 2006). The main complaint of these democracy promoters is that several governments subject to Western democracy promotion activities aimed at building and strengthening civil society have increasingly implemented restrictive legal codes and extra-legal forms of harassment against human rights and pro-democracy NGOs working in their countries, particularly those domestic groups receiving assistance from Western donors. Thus, foreign governments and organizations seeking to assist the development of civil society as an agent for democratic political change stand the chance of creating a contradictory situation by raising suspicions on the part of the host government, which may lead to a clampdown on civil society activity. This highlights an additional dynamic within the political context that shapes civil society's democratizing potential: the particular international circumstances within which the civil society promotion is taking place. Accordingly, one can posit, as the following analysis of U.S. activities in Cuba will show, that the more hostile the relationship between the democracy promoter and host government, and the more overt the nature of the promoter's civil society assistance is, the more leverage the host government may have to brand those groups receiving the foreign assistance as tools of foreign political interests, and thereby, use this to justify the repression of these groups.

6. Bottom-up: The Empirical Analysis

6.1. A Contentious, Cuban Civil Society

The Cuban Government boasts of a "socialist civil society" in Cuba that "comprises more than 2,200 organizations, some of the most prominent of which are the social and grassroot[s] organizations, and the technical, scientific, cultural, artistic, sports, friendship and solidarity organizations or associations, and any others which operate by virtue of the Associations Act (Law 54)" (Republic of Cuba, Ministry of Foreign Affairs 2008b). It sees Cuban civil society "as a complement and not in opposition to the state" (Ibid.). The United States Government on the other hand, views Cuban civil society as "weak," its development "impeded by pervasive and continuous [state] repression" (CAFC 2004, 15). The discrepancy between these two different observations attests to the ambiguous concept of civil society, particularly in its relationship vis-à-vis the state. Essentially, the discrepancy highlights the emphasis placed on civil society as a motor for democratization in non-democratic states; a force working to overturn the existing political system (Friedman 2004, 6). While the relationship between civil society and the state serves to highlight certain characteristics of civil society, this should not automatically imply an environment of isolation from, or hostility to, the state on the part of civil society (Dilla/Oxhorn 2002, 13). Mercer (2002, 7) suggests that by viewing civil society only in its autonomous role outside the state, observers fail to recognize the function of civil society as a potentially democratic sphere in its own right, through which alternative visions of democracy might be pursued.

The case of Cuba serves as an excellent example of competing conceptions and expectations of civil society's role vis-à-vis the state and its place within the process of democratization. The discussion surrounding the development of civil society in Cuba began during the 1990s as Cuban society was undergoing changes brought about by various government reforms that sought to deal with the economic hardships of the Special Period. The effect of these reforms was the development of a more relaxed space for professional and community groups to help implement state policies, which ultimately led to an increase in civic groups (Dilla/Oxhorn 2002, 15). As a consequence, various "mini-spheres" of discourse, not directed from the top-down, began appearing in the Cuban public sphere (Hoffmann/Whitehead 2006, 16). These changes were accompanied by an increasing debate among Cuban intellectuals and the Cuban state surrounding the significance of this new civil society and its compatibility within the socialist system. By the mid-1990s, however, the debate was brought to an end by the Cuban Government. In response to the Libertad Act's authorization for the funding of Cuban civil society organizations to promote a democratic transition in Cuba, the Cuban Government rashly denounced the concept of civil society as a "bourgeois conception;" a neoliberal "Trojan Horse;" a "fifth column . . . aimed at undermining socialist society from within" (cited in Dilla/Oxhorn 2002, 24). The state moved aggressively to restrict many of the recent organizations that had emerged, refused to grant legal recognition to newer groups, and increased its control over other NGOs. The Cuban Government then undertook the task of defining a "socialist civil society" consisting of organizations whose goals were compatible within the socialist system (Ibid., 25).

Law 54 of the Cuban Constitution of 1992 is used to regulate citizen organizations within the framework of the Cuban state. The law grants the rights of "assembly, demonstration, and association" to "workers, both manual and intellectual, peasants, women, students and other sectors of the working people" through the existing "social and mass organizations," which "have all the facilities . . . need[ed] to carry out those activities" (Constitution of the Republic of Cuba, 1992). Thus, the law emphasizes the existing state structures and their compatible organizations as the vehicles for citizen participation within the socialist system. The recognition of independent organizations in Cuba existing outside of these structures is dependent on the discretion of the Cuban Ministry of Justice for the granting of legal operational status. If such organizations are found acceptable, they are in turn subject to regulation and interference by the state, and thereby denied broad autonomy in their activities (NED 2006, 48).

The mass state-organizations, such as the Committees for the Defense of the Revolution (CDR), the Federation of Cuban Women (FMC), or the Central Cuban Workers' Organization (CTC), have several millions of members. They are often characterized as "conveyor belts" within the state's centralized system, serving to help implement state policies coming from above, while also providing a "feedback" function for communicating popular perceptions back to the state apparatus at the top (Ibid., 18; Bertelsmann Stiftung 2007, 10). At the same time, these organizations are also seen as providing Cubans with an important channel for civic communication and participation within the socialist system (Dilla/Oxhorn 2002, 17). The CDRs, for example, beyond their capacity as vigilant, ideological watchdogs, carry out responsibilities in the areas of health care, education, volunteer work, defense, citizen security, and social activities (Friedman 2004, 22, 23). Various other state organizations hosting smaller memberships, such as student and small farmer organizations or professional associations of artists, journalists, lawyers, and economists, regularly participate in decision-making and are capable of assuming various positions on those state policies that affect their sphere of activities (Dilla/Oxhorn 2002, 17, 18). At the local levels, Cuban community organizations are active in mobilizing citizen participation in policy discussions, mostly with the aim of better implementing the existing state policies, but also with the aim of influencing the government towards needed policy changes. Accordingly, the programs of these local organizations identify with the revolution's socialist system and anti-system goals are not found among the activist members (Domínguez 2000, 100). Rather than demanding the end of one-party rule, they pressure for new relationships with it, in order to improve government policies and their implementation (Dilla/Oxhorn 2002, 23).

In explaining this environment of civil society participation in Cuba, Dilla and Oxhorn (Ibid., 23) highlight the role of the Cuban state itself as a promoter of opportunities for the development of civil society, chiefly, by way of its social programs, which have led to the involvement of ordinary citizens in public activity. In fact, during the 1990s many Cuban NGOs argued to their European partners that the Cuban state's social objectives greatly resemble those of NGOs working in Western countries (Pearson/Lewis 1995, 18). Yet, due to its mistrust, the state limits the opportunity of autonomous association, thereby creating "a contradictory situation in which it [the state] is trying to restrict the opportunities for citizen action that it has itself made possible through its undeniable and commendable social commitment" (Dilla/Oxhorn 2002, 23).

Thus, the Cuban case demonstrates the problematic of understanding the growth and development of Cuban civil society only in the context of anti-regime, dissident groups and organizations (Pearson/Lewis 1995, 18). The unique characteristics of a developing Cuban civil society suggest a state regulated sphere, in which groups display not anti-system programs, but rather programs that identify with the revolution's social goals, with the aim of improving the functional quality of the existing system. The United States, on the other hand, defines Cuban civil society as only those groups in open opposition to the Cuban regime, while rejecting these other organizations that carry out important functions of civil society (Friedman 2004, 18). In fact, U.S. law prohibits direct assistance to any NGOs registered and recognized by the Cuban State due to their "control" and "interrelation" with the government (U.S. Agency for International Development 2006, 5; hereafter USAID). The only eligible candidates for the U.S. civil society programs, therefore, are the autonomous dissident and opposition organizations within Cuba. Such conceptions are also found within the academic community. For example, one scholar of Cuban civil society states: "The amount of political space molded by the internal opposition is a barometer to measure the strength of civil society in Cuba . . . " (Pumar 1999, 368). In fact, it is exactly this formula that is used by the U.S. Government to measure the growth and strength of Cuban civil society. The United States Agency for International Development (USAID) uses a "proxy SO indicator (public acts of Cuban civil society)" to measure the U.S. Government's objective of strengthening Cuban civil society and, thereby, its positive impact on promoting democracy in Cuba (USAID 2006, 5, 6). In other words, the more public acts of civil disobedience undertaken by groups in Cuba, the stronger the U.S. Government perceives Cuban civil society to be.

Cuban scholar Rafael Hernández has taken issue with foreign assumptions regarding the autonomy of Cuban civil society being suppressed by the government, and more importantly, the assumption that only dissidents and opposition activists in Cuba can be ordered into Cuban civil society. Firstly, he notes the contrast between the "anti-system" aims of these opposition groups and the aims of the semi-autonomous community organizations that work within the state system by mobilizing local citizens to improve and "better implement existing state programs" (cited in Domínguez 2000, 102). Secondly, he notes the contrast between the "external notoriety" of dissident and oppositional organizations "and their lack of any presence in Cuban civil society itself" (cited in Dilla/Oxhorn 2002, 22). Dilla and Oxhorn (Ibid.) describe these dissident groups in Cuba as numerous, but very small and unstable; their numbers exceeding no more than a few hundred and their influence minute:

[They] have little or no influence on national life, even at the local level . . . [They] are mostly made up of people who wish to immigrate to the United States, and this contributes to the instability of their organizations and membership . . . [Their] politics and proposals exhibit a remarkable degree of compatibility with U.S. policy toward Cuba, and this gives them an anti-national character that limits their mobilization capacity (22).

While their influence among the broader sphere of Cuban society is said to be trivial, the Cuban Government takes no chance that their influence may expand. The government permits a limited degree of space for the organizational activities of these groups, with the effect that it can better identify the existence of such groups and monitor their activities (NED 2006, 18). Oswaldo Payá, a moderate Cuban opposition leader, has commented that the more extreme dissident groups are regularly infiltrated and influenced by Cuban security agents (CNN International 2005). Furthermore, the activities of these groups are regulated by strict laws such as the Law for Protection of National Independence and the Economy of Cuba, a law penalizing counter-revolutionary or subversive activities (NED 2006, 48). On this note, it would be profitable to turn now to an analysis of the U.S. programs to promote civil society in Cuba, looking into the efficacy of these programs in contributing to their stated goal of promoting a democratic transition.

6.2. U.S. Promotion of Civil Society in Cuba

As previously discussed, during the 1980s the founding of the National Endowment For Democracy and the political lobbying efforts of the Cuban American National Foundation led to the development of overt activities to promote a transition to democracy in Cuba. These activities included propaganda efforts such as the broadcasting of Radio and TV Martí and other informational programs. With the Cuban Democracy Act and the Libertad Act during the 1990s, U.S. Cuba policy increasingly began focusing on the development of civil society in Cuba as a democratizing agent. This second flank in the U.S. policy established a channel for financial, technical, informational, and humanitarian assistance to NGOs and civil organizations in Cuba to promote "democracy-building efforts" on the island (Libertad, §109). Since 1984, NED has awarded over $13.3 million in grants to organizations with the aim of promoting democracy in Cuba (U.S. Government Accountability Office 2006, 3; hereafter USGAO). Following the passage of the Libertad Act these grants for democracy promotion activities in Cuba began going through USAID and reached a total sum of roughly $74 million by 2005 (Ibid.). As a result of President Bush's Cuba campaign, the annual amount of U.S. Government funds channeled through USAID to promote democracy in Cuba has most recently risen from $9 million annually to the massive figure of $45.7 million for 2008.

6.2.1. The Program

The aim of the USAID-Cuba program is to build and promote "civil society by increasing the flow of accurate information on democracy, human rights, and free enterprise to, from, and within Cuba" (USAID 2006, 4). The program consists of various types of on-island and off-island activities. There are projects aimed at providing various types of material support and assistance to on-island Cuban dissident groups such as computers, printers, fax machines, short-wave radios, food and medicine, as well as informational materials such as books, magazines, and DVDs. There are other projects which are aimed at "giving voice to Cuba's independent journalists," whereby reports written by Cubans are sent out of Cuba and published on news websites such as the Florida based CubaNet. These activities are complimented by programs that provide training courses for these independent journalists. Other programs are aimed at establishing independent libraries in Cuba, which offer information on human rights, democracy, and free markets. Cuban opposition organizations are provided with other various types of NGO management training as well as financial and material support to keep their organizations up and running and help support the families of group members serving jail sentences for their political activities. Lastly, numerous off-island activities take place at U.S. universities and think tanks, which include projects such as surveys of recent Cuban immigrants or Cuba "transition studies" that aim at planning for a post-transition, democratic Cuba (USAID 2005).

To carry out these various projects, the millions of dollars of USAID-Cuba funds go to three different types of grantees: democracy and human rights NGOs with a focus specifically on Cuba, groups with a worldwide or regional focus, and several universities and think tanks. Between 1996 and 2005, these grants went to a total of 34 organizations, all based in the United States (USGAO 2006, 15). The main groups in the U.S. democracy promotion apparatus such as Freedom House, NED, and its sister organizations such as the International Republican Institute and the National Democratic Institute (representing their U.S. political party counterparts) receive grants to undertake their own projects and also channel funds further along to smaller organizations. These smaller, more private democracy and human rights organizations are geared towards getting the material and financial assistance to groups on the island and also receive additional grants directly from USAID. Then there are the universities and think tanks, which receive hundreds of thousands of dollars for research and other academic activities (USAID 2005).[15]

According to a report by the Cuban American National Foundation (2008), out of all these activities undertaken in the USAID-Cuba program, only 46% of total USAID funds were allocated to the promotion of Cuban civil society between the years 1998 and 2006. In turn, the majority of these funds went to only four organizations based in the U.S., which together, used only 36% of their grants for the purchase and distribution of books, equipment, and humanitarian aid to groups in Cuba. The rest of the funds went into these organizations' operating costs. The remaining 54% of total USAID funds were distributed among the various think tanks and universities to undertake academic studies (Ibid., 3) such as the "Cuban Transition Project" at the Institute of Cuban and Cuban-American Studies in Miami, which has received roughly half a million dollars from USAID to help the U.S. Government plan for a political transition in Cuba (Bachelet 2008).

In addition to the activities of these organizations, the U.S. Government continues supporting the broadcasting efforts of Radio and TV Martí, which are run under the auspices of the Office of Cuba Broadcasting (OCB) in

---

[15] The main institutional characteristic within this community of quasi-private and private organizations is its revolving door feature, whereby actors are consistently traveling back and forth between the private and public sectors – positions within the U.S. Government, private corporations and firms, and the Republican and Democratic political parties – which often leads to overlapping leaderships between various organizations. This tight relationship of networks greatly explains the democracy promotion community's successful and continued subsistence on large amounts of U.S. taxpayer money.

Miami. Together these two programs receive a budget separate from the USAID-Cuba funds of roughly $40 million annually to broadcast over 300 hours weekly into Cuba (U.S. Department of State and the Broadcasting Board of Governors, Office of Inspector General 2007, 18; hereafter USDOS, OIG). Critics of the OCB have faulted the programs for decades on charges of bias and favoritism, arguing that the broadcasts generally omit any news that is critical of the U.S. policy and the Cuban exile community in favor of strict anti-Castro programming (Ibid., 7). Moreover, in 2003 an audit by the Office of the Inspector General documented several violations of government procurement regulations by the OCB. The report found that the OCB had been regularly awarding no-bid contracts and acting in other ways that suggested policies of favoritism (Ibid. 2003, 4). This seems congruent with the claims of some Cuban exiles that TV and Radio Martí serve primarily as a source of income for the well-connected Miami exiles (Goodnough 2006). Among the most criticized aspect of the program, however, is the fact that the Cuban Government routinely jams the signals of both Radio and TV Martí broadcasts (USDOS, OIG 2003, 9).

Like the programs running at the OCB, the USAID-Cuba program has also been subject to much public criticism, particularly in the last several years. As the Commission for Assistance to a Free Cuba was recommending raising the annual congressional appropriations to promote civil society and democracy in Cuba to $47.1 million annually, the USAID-Cuba program became the subject of several unraveling scandals. In 2006 the U.S. Government Accountability Office (GAO) conducted an audit of the program on request of the U.S. Congress. The investigation found that out of the $74 million in program grants awarded since 1996, 95% ($61.9 million) of these had been awarded in response to unsolicited proposals with no bidding and no public notice of program proposals (USGAO 2006, 3). Furthermore, the audit uncovered a lack of program monitoring and oversight on the part of USAID to provide assurance that the funds were being used properly.

While USAID took pride and commended itself on the amount of assistance the program had gotten into the hands of Cubans since 1996 – 385,000 pounds of medicines, food and clothing; more than 23,000 short-wave radios; and millions of books and newsletters, – the GAO audit uncovered other items the grants had been used for, which USAID had failed to mention. Among these were purchases by various grantees including "a gas chainsaw, computer gaming equipment and software (including Nintendo Gameboys and Sony Playstations), a mountain bike, leather coats, cashmere sweaters, crab meat and Godiva chocolates" (USGAO 2006, 37). The GAO report made its way into the debates of the 2007 congressional appropriations session tasked with authorizing the massive increase in new funds for the Cuba program. One congressman argued that "to increase [USAID-Cuba] funding to almost $50 million, or by about 500 percent, is not just irresponsible, it has an Alice in wonderland quality about it" (U.S. House of Representatives 2007a, E6835). "What do Godiva chocolates have to do with promoting democracy in Cuba?" questioned another representative (Ibid.). This rhetorical question was answered by Juan Carlos Acosta, executive director of the Miami-based group *Acción Democrática Cubana* (Cuban Democratic Action), responsible for purchasing several of the contested items: "These people [Cubans] are going hungry," Acosta explained, "they never get any chocolate there [in Cuba]" (Luscombe 2006). Another organization, *Grupo de Apoyo a la Democracia* (Groups for the Support of Democracy), defended its purchase of several boxes of computer games with part of its $7 million USAID grant as "part of our job, to show the people in Cuba what they could have if they were not under that system" (Ibid.).

In spite of the incompetence and mismanagement of several grantees revealed by the GAO audit, the U.S. Congress approved the increase in aid to $45.7 million. In turn, the warnings emphasized in the GAO report were ignored, which led to another scandal less than a year later. In March 2008, the Cuban American National Foundation undertook a study of the USAID-Cuba program, concluding that it "has been rendered utterly ineffective due to . . . [the] lack of oversight and accountability of grantee recipients" (CANF 2008, 2). The report found the amount of aid actually reaching groups on the island to be miniscule. Less than 17% of all USAID-Cuba funds distributed between 1998 and 2006 had been used for "direct, on-island assistance," while the remaining 83% of these funds went to the "operating expenses of grantee organizations, off-island transition studies and U.S. based activities" (Ibid.).

Only a month after the release of the CANF study, further audits of the USAID-Cuba program grantees uncovered massive fraud. In May 2008, just as USAID was about to release the $45.7 million in new grants, White House Special Assistant to the President, Felipe Sixto, resigned his position amid allegations of defrauding the USAID-Cuba program of more than half a million dollars when he worked for the Center for a Free Cuba, a Cuban American organization heavily subsidized by USAID (Associated Press 2008b). In the mists of this newest scandal, the audits uncovered another case of fraud involving the head of *Grupo de Apoyo a la Democracia*, who had spent tens of thousands of dollars in grant money on "personal items" (Associated Press 2008c). Although the continuous scandals led the House Foreign Affairs Committee to freeze the new USAID-Cuba grants in June 2008, they were unfrozen less than a month later upon promises by the State Department and USAID that they would improve the program's auditing and review process (Ibid.).

In sum, the USAID-Cuba program displays more the characteristics of a government-subsidized cottage industry for organizations in Florida and

Washington than a program aimed at assisting civil society in Cuba. In fact, the public spectacle emerging around the USAID-Cuba program in the last years has led to new efforts to channel the program grants to foreign NGOs, particularly in Eastern Europe, for the purpose of promoting democracy in Cuba. Jose Cardenas, former member of CANF and the new head of the Cuba program at USAID, has said that getting the aid to Central European and Latin American NGOs will help U.S. efforts to promote democracy because of these groups' experience in organizing opposition groups in authoritarian societies. "They know how to evade the authoritarian government's efforts to control your behavior," he explains (Richter 2008). While this new shift towards getting the funds to foreign NGOs may be partly understood by the incompetence of several U.S. organizations and their wasteful use of U.S. taxpayer money, the reorientation reflects more so the increasing problem involved in the U.S. Government's role in financing and assisting the activities of dissident groups in Cuba. A brief account of the program's impact on the island should make this last point clear.

6.2.2. The Impact

As pointed out earlier, the United States Government funds only those organizations in Cuba that operate autonomously from the Cuban state, and are likewise subject to much suspicion by the Cuban Government. These groups can be punished in Cuba under Law 88, the Law for the Protection of National Independence and the Economy of Cuba, which sentences persons for up to 20 years for counterrevolutionary and subversive activities that involve any support for, or actions that help enforce, the United State's Libertad Act (NED 2006, 40; Bond 2003, 120). Dissident activists can also be sentenced under Article 91 of the Cuban Penal Code, which subjects those "who [undertake] an action in the interest of a foreign state with the purpose of harming the independence of the Cuban state or the integrity of its territory . . . [to] a sentence of 10 to 20 years of deprivation of liberty or death" (Pérez Roque 2003). Thus, It is a balancing act of U.S. policy to support and assist the growth and activities of these oppositional organizations on the one hand, while not subjecting them to repression from the Cuban Government for their collaboration with the United States on the other.

Due to the illegal nature of these groups under Cuban laws, a large part of the material and financial assistance coming from the United States must be smuggled into the country. Hence, this assistance is constantly subject to loss due to confiscations by the Cuban Government (USGAO 2006, 4). The U.S. Interests Section in Havana, therefore, plays an important role in delivering the majority of this assistance to groups on the island. Complete with its own printing press, the Interests Section distributes a daily newspaper and several magazines, as well as many of the items arriving from the U.S. such as the books, newspapers, videos, shortwave radios, computers, and DVD players. The office also maintains regular contact with opposition groups and activists on the island. It provides Internet access and other means of long-distance communication as well as training courses for oppositional organizations in several areas of NGO organization (Ibid., 13). In general, the U.S. Interests Section seems to function as the operations base between the groups on the island and the assistance coming from the U.S., much of which is brought into Cuba as diplomatic baggage (Pérez Roque 2003). It is, therefore, no surprise that the Cuban Government has raised extreme concern over the Interests Sections' activities. Most recently the Cuban Government charged the office of delivering large amounts of hard cash directly to dissidents in Cuba to carry out their opposition work, accusing it of actively "encouraging, financing, organizing, directing, and carefully monitoring the cover of provocative activities by mercenaries [opposition groups] to destabilize the country's internal order" (Granma International 2008).

In fact, it was these overt activities, heightened by the arrival in Havana of James Cason in September 2002 to head the U.S. Interests Section, which led up to the Cuban Government's 2003 arrest and imprisonment of 75 Cuban dissidents. During Cason's time at the office he displayed an aggressive and defiant attitude in his activities in Cuba and is thought to have greatly antagonized the Cuban Government by working closer with Cuban opposition groups than any previous Interests Section diplomat, even opening his Havana home for meetings with numerous Cuban dissidents (Bond 2003, 121, 122; Craig 2007, 366). The Cuban Government had in fact issued several complaints with the Interests Section and the State Department, but the activities continued. Thus, during two days in March 2003 Cuban security forces moved in on the groups that had reportedly been meeting with Cason and other U.S. officials. Among those arrested, for example, were 27 of the U.S. assisted independent journalists, 14 librarians from 22 of the U.S. supported independent libraries, and numerous others involved in active opposition groups (Freedom House 2007).

Following the broad international disapproval of the arrests carried out by the Cuban Government, Cuban Foreign Minister Pérez Roque, in an effort to justify the repression, held a press conference presenting some of the evidence used during the trials of those arrested. The evidence presented by the foreign minister consisted of confirmation letters and receipts detailing payments made to Cuban dissidents through USAID and NED financed organizations. In the house of one independent journalist, for example, Cuban authorities reportedly found over $7,000 hidden in the lining of a suit and several receipts detailing payments the activist had received from the USAID supported CubaNet news website in Miami (Pérez Roque 2003).

Several other financial receipts confiscated in the raids documented the delivery of money to persons in Cuba from various organizations in the U.S. According to Pérez Roque (Ibid.), "in the work carried out prior to the trials tens of thousands of [U.S.] dollars were seized" from those arrested. Other materials confiscated by authorities and presented as court evidence included detailed lists of material items from U.S. organizations that had been smuggled into the country for dissidents such as televisions, VCRs, lamps, an electric stove, "a set of pots and pans," and food and medicines. The foreign minister also presented several court testimonies of Cuban security agents who had infiltrated the Cuban organizations as dissidents in order to uncover the networks built around the U.S. Interests Section. One Cuban undercover agent, posing as a dissident and working as an independent journalist for CubaNet, described how he met with representatives at the Interests Section, who would outline to him the pertinent subjects he should be writing about such as "the food shortage . . ., the blackouts . . ., the transport situation, the lack of medicines" and so forth, which would then be published abroad on foreign websites (Ibid.).

It should come as no surprise that those arrested were accused of working as paid agents of the United States and tried under Law 88 for conspiring to subvert the Cuban Government (NED 2006, 40; Bond 2003, 120). It is, however, most important to note that a bias on the part of Cuban security forces and Cuban courts was clearly displayed during the arrests and sentencing of the 75 dissidents. Those groups most closely associated with the U.S. Interests Section faced more arrests and received more severe sentences than those groups that had kept their distance from the U.S. sponsored activities (Craig (2007).

6.3. Throwing a Boomerang

As this chapter shows, there are several flaws existing in the U.S. policy to promote civil society as an agent of democratization in Cuba. In general, the U.S. activities in Cuba seem to have the effect of hindering such a development more than encouraging it. Firstly, very little of the millions of dollars in USAID grants seem to even make it into the hands of groups in Cuba. The majority of the funds are siphoned off through the numerous democracy promotion organizations in Washington and Florida to pay for operational costs, the production of speculative "transition studies" for a post-Castro Cuba, and, among other questionable purchases, predetermined news reports from Cuban dissidents.

Secondly, the U.S. assistance to dissident groups that does reach the island allows the Cuban Government to move against these groups and charge them with conspiring to overthrow the Cuban Government. A former U.S. diplomat to Cuba, Wayne Smith, has summed up the consequences of the program superbly: "It's like putting a target on the back of their heads when you say your objective is to bring down the [Cuban] government and one of your means of doing so is to give assistance to the dissidents in Cuba. That's turning them, for all to see, into paid agents of a foreign government" (cited in Sanchez 2008). In fact, several groups in Cuba have criticized the U.S. policy as harmful for those groups working for change in Cuba that do not identify with the U.S. policy. Oswaldo Payá, for example, leader of the Varela Project, has long been a critic of U.S. Government policy towards Cuba and refuses to accept aid from the U.S. Interests Section (Craig 2007, 366).[16] Mariam Leiva of Ladies in White has also stated her position of being "against any funds from the American Government." The main consequence of these funds, she explains, "is that it gives the Cuban Government a pretext to say that we are mercenaries and put us in jail" (cited in U.S. House of Representatives 2007a, H6835).

Finally, by failing to take into account the dynamic situation of civil society in Cuba and assisting mainly those groups with an anti-system agenda, the U.S policy serves to fuel the Cuban Government's mistrust of independent organizations in general, perhaps more so than would be in the absence of the U.S. threat. The policy, therefore, provides the government with justification for clamping down on the autonomy of all organizations in order to avoid the development of a U.S. supported and U.S. directed civil society; a neo-liberal "Trojan horse." In turn, this directly weakens the growth and maneuverability of those civil society organizations seeking to work within the system for more moderate change in Cuba. These groups, particularly the community organizations, which identify with the socialist agenda, are indeed focused on issues such as decentralization and other possibilities of reform that could lead to the better implementation of government policies. While these groups are limited in autonomy, they are not without influence in local debates concerning state policies, and they signal a semi-democratic participative sphere of action in there own right. This could potentially lead to even more democratic forms of citizen participation within the socialist framework of the Cuban state (Domínguez 2000, 101). However, to promote the important components of Cuban civil society that identify and work with the socialist state would be to recognize the social aims of the Cuban Government instead of helping build opposi-

---

[16] The Varela Project was a referendum initiative in Cuba. In 2002 the project submitted more than 11,000 signatures to the Cuban National Assembly demanding a referendum to let Cubans vote on fundamental reforms such as freedom of expression, the right to own private businesses, and electoral reform. The proposal was rejected by a constitutional committee and the government then held a counter referendum, gathering 8.2 million signatures declaring the socialist system to be "untouchable" (Freedom House, 2007).

tion to these aims and thereby furthering the U.S. project of promoting democracy in Cuba via regime change.

To turn back to the comment of former Assistance Secretary of State for Western Hemisphere Affairs Noriega at the beginning of chapter 5, he stated that the U.S. embargo "supports the development of civil society" by denying the Cuban Government the means to "strengthen its repressive apparatus" and suppress civil society (U.S. Senate, Committee on Foreign Relations 2003, 73). Noriega's view fails to grasp this dynamic situation of civil society in Cuba. The U.S. policy, with the embargo as its central piece, does not weaken the Cuban state's ability to repress political dissent, but instead, provides a rational for it. His analysis is grounded in the conception of civil society as a motor for democratization – civil society versus the non-democratic state. It is supported by particular historical readings such as the successful struggle of the Solidarnosc movement in Poland, which was greatly supported by U.S. assistance. His commentary takes into account neither the unique situation of civil society as it exists in Cuba nor the consequences of U.S. assistance to those groups it deems Cuban civil society. The observation of one Cuba commentator at the Washington-based Center for International Policy sums up the quagmire resulting from the premise underlying the U.S. strategy to assist Cuban civil society to promote a transition to democracy: "It worked in Poland because the adversary of Polish nationalism was the Soviet Union, but in Cuba the adversary of Cuban nationalism is the United States" (Fox News 2003).

7. Conclusion: The Anatomy of Folly

This analysis of the U.S. Cuba policy has uncovered several weaknesses in the potential of both its top-down and bottom-up approaches to promote democracy in Cuba. In fact, the policy seems to be less a strategy to promote a democratic transition than a strategy aimed merely at the destruction of a non-democratic regime. Returning to the questions raised in the introduction regarding the theoretical underpinnings of the U.S. policy, the evidence suggests the following insights. While economic failure may bring about certain political dynamics leading to authoritarian breakdown, the use of economic sanctions – not only ethically questionable in the case of U.S. Cuba policy – may, within the particular international context, produce effects that counteract these internal dynamics. Furthermore, while civil society is an important – but not exclusive – contributor to regime breakdown and democratization, the external promotion of civil society, depending on the specific international context, may well worsen, rather than improve, the internal political environment that shapes the democratization potential of civil society. It does this by pushing non-democratic regimes to further close off avenues favorable to the development of civil society as a motor for democratization.

Supporting these deductive conclusions are, of course, the malfunctioning structures within the U.S. policy to promote a democratic transition in Cuba, indentified in chapters 4 and 6. They can now be briefly recapitulated. Regarding the top-down strategy, the U.S. attempt to bring about the dynamics of poor economic performance and regime breakdown has pushed the Cuban Government into neither a crisis of legitimacy nor instability – two important factors within authoritarian breakdown discussed in chapter 3. This is due to several factors. First and foremost is the factor of unilateral coercion. The Cuban Government has proven very adept at dodging the impact of the U.S. sanctions by strategically reorienting and adapting its economy and trade to the changing circumstances of the global economy. Although the economic performance of the Cuban regime and the general economic wellbeing of its citizens have, at times, suffered serious setbacks, the degree of economic destruction that the U.S. policy is aimed at has clearly not emerged.

This failure is also related to a second factor resulting from the poor co-ordination within the U.S. policy. Cuban victims of economic hardship and disaffection – to whatever degree the sanctions are or are not responsible – are relieved of this by the liberal U.S. policy on Cuban migration. An important premise in the U.S. top-down approach, of course, is that economic disaffection will stir popular opposition among Cubans against the regime and bring the government under increased pressure from below. The U.S. Cuban migration policy, however, allows disaffected Cubans to vote with their feet and not their voice. Thus, by removing possible political opposition from inside Cuba, the United States is preempting the development of internal pressures which could begin chipping away at the Cuban regime's legitimacy and stability. In fact, the legitimacy and stability of the Cuban regime is to a great extent assisted by a third factor of U.S. policy: the continuance of the embargo. This last factor, as Hoffmann (2001b, 11) points out, "could scarcely be more helpful for the strategy of the Cuban Government to recast every internal struggle into the dichotomous friend-enemy schema of 'Cuba versus the United States'." As a result, the sanctions offer the regime an extra source of performance legitimacy based not on economic performance, but on protecting Cuban sovereignty from the designs of the United States.

As was also discussed in chapter 3, the structure of failed economic performance alone does not bring about regime collapse, but rather the actions and reactions of elite actors are a deciding factor in regime breakdown and democratic transition. This dynamic, of course, entails rational decision-making among actors, which is largely influenced by the options and incentives available to them. Within this context, a fourth factor of U.S. policy can be identified that underlies its failure to bring about a democratic transition in Cuba. The policy fails to encourage reform-oriented shifts within Havana's internal, political power-constellation by significantly limiting the options, and thereby incentives, for democratic political change. As long as the criteria for a transition government and a democratically elected government in Cuba remain strictly defined by the Libertad Act, and members of the Cuban Government and Cuban Communist Party are discriminated against by Washington, any moves toward democratization and the normalization of relations with the U.S. will remain off-limits to Cuban officials dedicated to protecting Cuban sovereignty and independence – not to mention their livelihoods.

Although for analytical purposes the top-down and bottom-up strategies have been dealt with separately in this study, they are explicitly linked to one another. Not only does the top-down approach close off routes to democratic political change from above, but it also undermines the bottom-up strategy of promoting oppositional civil society groups in Cuba. U.S. policy allows the regime in Havana to delegitimize the aims of these groups while also providing it with an excuse to move repressively against them. As an indirect consequence of this dynamic, Sweig (2007, 52) notes, Cubans have come to "regard Washington not as a beacon of freedom against tyranny but as an imperialist oppressor that has helped justify domestic repression." The evidence presented in chapter 6 clearly shows that the U.S. activities to promote Cuban civil society (i.e. dissident activity), beyond creating a well-subsidized cottage industry in the United States for well-connected Cuban exiles, does little to help Cuban attempts at building a civil society that can interact with the Cuban state in positive ways. The U.S. policy pushes the reactionary moves on the side of the Cuban Government to keep all routes closed through which U.S. intervention may occur. It therefore delays the growth of a social sphere outside of state control, within which an autonomous Cuban civil society can develop and provide a legitimate, domestic challenge to the legitimacy of the Cuban regime.

Together, both approaches of the U.S. strategy have created structures that do more to prevent, rather than promote, the goal of democratic transformation in Cuba. Whitehead (2002, 86) describes the strategy as having the effect of a "blunt" instrument, which "may . . . damage rather than build up the social supports for democracy." By aiming specifically at regime change and an end to the socialist state, U.S. policy continues to encourage the internal hardening and coherence of the Cuban regime. Just as the aggressive U.S. response to the Cuban Revolution helped push the development of a tightly controlled bureaucratic, non-democratic Cuban state fifty years ago, the continuation of the hostile confrontation ensures the continuation of the Cuban Government's non-democratic character. It is precisely the U.S. resolve to escalate economic costs and encourage internal political division and unrest in Cuba that reinforces the authoritarian tendencies on the part of the Cuban central government to close off avenues that could encourage peaceful, democratic processes of political change (Hoffmann 2001b, 10).

The failure of the U.S. policy to bring about the collapse of the Cuban Government and its negative counterproductive consequences on promoting democracy in Cuba is clear. Cuban democracy activist Miriam Leiva puts it bluntly: "If it [U.S. Government] wants to help the Cuban people, it should lift the embargo and allow trade, tourism, and academic exchanges, and Cubans should be allowed to travel without restriction to the United States and send money to their families [in Cuba]" (cited in House of Representatives 2007a, H6835). Since the mid-1990s, numerous legislation has been introduced in the U.S. Congress seeking to overturn Washington's failed embargo policy and replace it with a policy better inclined to promote democratic change in Cuba. In 2007, for example, House Representatives Rangel and Lee introduced the "Free Trade With Cuba Act." The proposed bill recognized both the "counterproductive" nature of the embargo and the hypocrisy of the U.S. Government in "using economic, cultural, academic, and scientific engagement to support its policy of promoting democratic and human rights reforms" in states such as China and Vietnam, while pursuing a strategy of isolation and aggression against Cuba (Ibid., 2007b). The act would repeal both the CDA and Libertad acts and require the U.S. president to conduct negotiations with the Cuban Government on property claims and respect for human rights. Like all other congressional initiatives to reform U.S. policy toward Cuba, however, the legislation was referred to several congressional subcommittees where it died.

If the U.S. policy serves not to promote democracy in Cuba, but rather to encourage authoritarian tendencies on the side of the Cuban Government, then what explains its obstinate continuance? Galtung (1967) reminds us that sanctions may be implemented out of the mere desire to punish a target country. The clear failure of the U.S. policy suggests that this may be one of the few factors driving it. Indeed, as President Bush (2001) highlighted during the commencement of his administration's Cuba campaign, the embargo is seen as more than "just a policy tool," it is "a moral statement." Deputy Assistant Secretary of State Daniel W. Fisk (2002) reaffirmed the need to punish Cuba, highlighting the obligation of the United States to "continue to signal our disapproval of Mr. Castro's rule and deny him the means of holding on to power." The grounds for this punishment, of course, arose with the Cuban Revolution's successful negation of the dominant U.S. hemispheric policy of more than a century: the Monroe Doctrine. To add insult to injury, the Cuban Revolution resulted in a communist state with close relations to the Soviet Union, thereby also negating the U.S. doctrine of Soviet containment. When both of these challenges to U.S. foreign policy simultaneously "came together and intersected in Cuba," Bernell (1994, 72) highlights, they proved to be "a highly volatile combination." With the end of the Cold War, the decades-long U.S. policy of containing Soviet-induced communism came to an end. The U.S. policy of punishing Cuba, however, did not. This is because the U.S. self-understanding of its hegemonic role in the Western Hemisphere did not abate with the end of the Cold War (Ibid., 96). The Cuban regime continues to defy this hegemonic presumption. It survived the invigorated attack of the U.S. Libertad Act, and the smooth transition from Fidel to Raúl Castro has now defied the new Bush strategy. This continued defiance results in continued punishment. Like a father scolding his misbehaving child, the U.S. Government makes clear to Cubans that obedience will be rewarded and continued disobedience punished. "The people of Cuba have a choice," reads the Bush Administration's *Compact with the People of Cuba*, "economic and political freedom and opportunity or more political repression and economic suffering under the current regime" (CAFC 2006c).

It can also not be overlooked that the continuation of the failed U.S. policy is unquestionably maintained by the considerable domestic rewards it reaps. In fact, the importance of the state of Florida in U.S. presidential elections may be the primary obstacle to reforming the U.S. policy (Staten 2003, 135). While the resolute U.S. policy may achieve the goals of signaling disapproval and pleasing certain domestic constituencies, its inherent feature that allows for determinant U.S. influence in shaping any 'transition government' or 'democratically elected government' that may come to power in Cuba may well serve as the main explanation of the policy's continuance. During a press conference on U.S. Cuba policy in 2002, Deputy Assistant Secretary Fisk (2002) pointed out the importance of this aspect of the policy:

> The question before us . . . is not whether to lift the restrictions on trade and tourism but when and how. Does it make any sense to hand a political victory and capital windfall to a hostile dictator in his final days who is the single biggest obstacle to genuine economic and political change? Or, does it make more sense to retain the leverage that we can use with a transition government to ensure deep and broad political and economic reform?

This leverage is the criterion laid out in Libertad, which promises a strong influential role for the United States in dictating the policy choices of any "democratically elected government" in Cuba that seeks to free itself from the U.S. embargo and normalize relations with Washington.

United States policy makers regularly take great care in articulating their Cuba policy rhetoric in terms that suggest the benevolence of the U.S. policy to help Cubans construct democracy. At the outset of his new Cuba initiative, President Bush (2002) sought to make clear that the United States "has no designs on Cuban sovereignty." Likewise, CAFC's 2006 *Report to the President* explained: "For all Cubans, we must underscore that the future is theirs to define" (18). A century ago, the U.S. Congress also sought to clarify to Cubans that the United States possessed no "intention to exercise sovereignty . . . or control over" their country (U.S. Congress 1898). The Platt Amendment, however, proved otherwise. Equally, the Libertad Act suggests otherwise. Indeed, when U.S. Cuba Transition Coordinator Caleb McCarry reaffirmed in 2006 that it is "the Cuban people [who] have to define their future," he subsequently made clear that this was not wholly the case: "[T]here are matters that are very important, and that are fundamental, and which we [U.S.] will not compromise . . .; they're laid out in our law [Libertad]" (USDOS 2006).

Matters such as returning expropriated property to U.S. citizens and the development of a capitalist economy in Cuba lie at the heart of Washington's push for democratization. The policy embodies the U.S. desire to have its way regarding the establishment and development of a political and economic environment in Cuba that is preferable to the United States. This need prompted the Platt Amendment in 1901, it justified U.S. support for dictators like Batista, and it also encouraged the aggressive U.S. response to the Cuban Revolution, prompting massive economic coercion, covert destabilization actions, assassination attempts on government leaders, and even a military invasion. These actions aimed at overthrowing a government the United States disliked in order to "bring about . . . a new [Cuban] government favorable to U.S. interests," as the Eisenhower Administration had so quickly planned (USDOS 1991, 742).

Thus, the U.S. policy seems to be more than just a relic of the Cold War. While the policy instruments used to promote democracy in Cuba – economic destruction and provocation of internal opposition – are a product of the Cold War, the policy's underlying ambition is a relic of 1898. In 1901, Senator Orville Platt, father of the Platt Amendment, justified the privilege of the United States to intervene in the internal affairs of Cuba as such: "We became responsible to the people of Cuba, to ourselves, and the world at large that a good government should be established and maintained in place of the bad one to which we put an end." "Our work," the senator continued, "was only half done when Cuba was liberated from its oppressor" (citied in Pérez 1999, 370). Today, the United States continues to hold itself responsible for the task of establishing 'a good government' in Cuba to replace the 'bad one' that, in the words of President George W. Bush (2002), "hijacked" Cuba's "independence . . . nearly half a century ago." As Schoultz (2002, 423) suggests, U.S. policy equates "good" with "democratic," while also monopolizing the definition of both terms. Since 1898 the United States has dictated to Cuba what is, and what is not, acceptable, all the while denying Cubans a fair chance to establish a democratic government by their own accord. Thus, while professing its strong commitment to the right of Cubans to self-determination, the United States, by acting on its perceived obligation to self-determine developments in Cuba to fit its own preference, ultimately denies that right to Cubans. Perhaps if the United States would end its paternalistic behavior, the Cuban state, no longer threatened by a foreign power that explicitly aims to destroy it, might, in time, democratize itself on its own terms.

References

Alarcón, Ricardo de Quesada. 2006. "Chronicle of a war foretold." *Granma*. July 5. <http://embacu.cubaminrex.cu/Default.aspx?tabid=7419> (Accessed 02.06.08).

Allen, Susan Hannah. 2008. "The Domestic Political Costs of Economic Sanctions." *Journal of Conflict Resolution* 52: 916-944.

American Journal of International Law. 1910. "Treaty between the United States and Cuba." 4(2), Supplement: Official Documents: 177-180.

Associated Press. 2008a. "Bush: Fidel Castro brother, apparent successor is 'dictator-lite.'" Feb. 19. Via NY Daily News. <http://www.foxnews.com/story/0,293 3,331154,00.html> (Accessed 12.08.08).

Associated Press. 2008b. "Bush aide resigns over misuse of money in Cuban democracy organization." Mar. 28. Via NY Daily News. <http://www.nydaily news. com/latino/2008/03/28/2008-03-28_bush_aide_resigns_over_misuse_of_ money_i.html> (Accessed 16.05.08).

Associated Press. 2008c. "US aid to Cuba unfrozen, State Department pledges reform." July 23. Via NY Daily News. <http://www.nydailynews.com/latino/2008 /07/23/2008-07-23_us_aid_to_cuba_unfrozen_state_dep_pledge-2.html> (Accessed 01.08.08).

Bachelet, Pablo. 2008. "U.S. shifting funds away from Miami anti-Castro groups." *The Miami Herald*. March 30. Via International Republican Institute. <http:// www.iri.org/newsarchive/2008/2008-03-30-News-MiamiHerald-Cuba.asp> (Accessed 03.08.08).

Bernell, David. 1994. "The Curious Case of Cuba in American Foreign Policy." *Journal of Inter-American Studies and World Affairs* 36(2): 65-103.

Bertelsmann Stiftung. 2007. *BTI 2008: Cuba Country Report*. Gütersloh: Bertelsmann Stiftung. <http://www.bertelsmann-transformation-index.de/95.0.html? &L=1> (Accessed 12.05.08).

Biox, Carles and Susan C. Stokes. 2003. "Endogenous Democratization." *World Politics* 55: 517-549.

Birle, Peter. 2000. "Zivilgesellschaft in Südamerika – Mythos und Realität." In Wolfgang Merkel (ed.). *Systemwechsel 5: Zivilgesellschaft und Transformation*. Opladen: Leske & Budrich: 231-272.

Bond, Theresa. 2003. "The Crackdown in Cuba." *Foreign Affairs* 82(5): 118-130.

Bremmer, Ian. 2006. *The J Curve*. New York: Simon & Schuster.

Brenner, Philip, Patrick J. Haney and Walter Vanderbush. 2004. "Intermestic Interests and U.S. Policy Toward Cuba." In Eugene R. Whitekopf and James M. McCormick (eds.). *The Domestic Sources of American Foreign Policy: Insights and Evidence*. Fourth edn. Oxford: Rowman and Littlefield Publishers: 67-83.

Bueno de Mesquita, Bruce and George W. Downs. 2005. "Development and Democracy." *Foreign Affairs* 84(5): 77-86.

Burnell, Peter. 2004. "Democracy Promotion: The Elusive Quest for Grand Strategies." *Internationale Politik und Gesellschaft* 4: 100-116.

Bush, George W. 2001. "Toward a Democratic Cuba." *State Department Press Release*. July 13. <http://www.state.gov/p/wha/rls/rm/2001/4301.htm> (Accessed 15.08.08).

Bush, George W. 2002. "President Bush Announces Initiative for a New Cuba." *White House Press Release*. May 20. <http://www.whitehouse.gov/news/releases/2002/05/20020520-1.html> (Accessed 15.08.08).

Bush, George W. 2006. "Cuba: Statement by President Bush." *White House Press Release*. Aug. 3. <http://www.state.gov/p/wha/rls/prsrl/2006/q3/69940.htm> (Accessed 31.07.08).

Bush, George W. 2007. "Remarks by the President on Cuba Policy." *White House Press Release*. Oct. 24. <http://www.state.gov/p/wha/rls/rm/07/q4/93965.htm> (Accessed 12.11.07).

Bush, George W. 2008. "Text of a Letter from the President to the Chairmen and Ranking Members of the House and Senate Committees of Appropriations, the House Committee on Foreign Affairs, and the Senate Committee on Foreign Relations." *White House Press Release*. Jan. 16. <http://www.whitehouse.gov/news/releases/2008/01/20080116-4.html> (Accessed 03.06.08).

Carothers, Thomas. 2007. *U.S. Democracy Promotion During and After Bush*. Washington DC: Carnegie Endowment for International Peace.

Carothers, Thomas. 2009. "Democracy Promotion Under Obama: Finding a Way Forward." *Carnegie Endowment for International Peace*. <http://www.carnegie endowment.org/files/democracy_promotion_obama.pdf> (Accessed 14.05.09).

Castro, Raúl. 2009. "Speech given by General of the Army Raúl Castro Ruz, President of the Councils of State and Ministers, during the 3rd ordinary session of the 7th Legislature of the National Assembly of People's Power, at the International Conference Center." *Gramna International*. Aug. 1. <http://www.granma.cu/ingles/2009/agosto/lun3/32raul-ing.html> (Accessed on 28.08.09).

CBS News. 2004. "U.N. condemns U.S. Cuba embargo." Oct. 28. <http://www.cbs news.com/stories/2004/11/30/world/main658417.shtml> (Accessed 31.07.08).

Chan, Steve and A. Cooper Drury. 2000. "Sanctions as Economic Statecraft: An Overview." In Steve Chan and A. Cooper Drury (eds.). *Sanctions as Economic Statecraft: Theory and Practice*. London: Macmillian Press: 1-16.

Clagett, Brice M. 1996. "Title III of the Helms-Burton Act is Consistent with International Law." *The American Journal of International Law* 90(3): 434-440.

CNN International. 2005. "Cuban dissidents rally in Havana." May 20. <http://edition.cnn.com/2005/WORLD/americas/05/20/cuba.rally/index.html> (Accessed 12.08.08).

Constitution of the Republic of Cuba, 1992. Via CubaNet News. <http://www.cuba net.org/ref/dis/const_92_e.htm> (Accessed 14.08.08).

Contreras, Joe. 2008. "Castro's successor promises change for a deeply troubled Cuba." *Newsweek*. Feb. 24. <http://www.newsweek.com/id/114942> (Accessed 02.05.09).

Craig, Matthew. 2007. "Making Sense of Dissidence and Repression In Cuba: A Game Theoretical Analysis." In *Cuba in Transition: Volume 17*. Washington DC: The Association for the Study of the Cuban Economy: 365-375.

Creighton University School of Law and Department of Political Science. 2007. *Report On The Resolution Of Outstanding Property Claims Between Cuba and The United States*. Omaha: Creighton University Press.

Croissant, Aurel, Hans-Joachim Lauth and Wolfgang Merkel. 2000. "Zivilgesellschaft und Transformation: ein internationaler Vergleich." In Wolfgang Merkel (ed.). *Systemwechsel 5: Zivilgesellschaft und Transformation*. Opladen: Leske & Budrich: 9-49.

Cuba Source. 2004. "Chronicle on Cuba – March 2004." The Canadian Foundation for the Americas. <http://www.cubasource.org/publications/chronicles/coc2004 03ex_e.asp> (Accessed 28.07.08).

Cuba versus Blockade. 2006. "Victory against U.S. blockade." Nov. 9. <http://www. cubavsbloqueo.cu/Default.aspx?tabid=1541> (Accessed 31.06.08).

Cuban American National Foundation. 2008. *Findings and Recommendations on the Most Effective Use of USAID-CUBA Funds Authorized by Section 109 (a) of the Cuban Liberty and Democratic Solidarity (Helms-Burton) Act of 1996*. March. <www.canf.org> (Accessed 16.05.08).

Cuban Democracy Act of 1992. Title 22 U.S. Code, Ch. 69, Sec. 6001-6010.

Dauderstädt, Michael and Marika Lerch. 2005. "International Democracy Promotion: Patiently Redistributing Power." *Internationale Politikanalyse*. May. Bonn: Friedrich Ebert Stiftung. <http://library.fes.de/pdf-files/id/02847. pdf> (Accessed 03.02.08).

Diamond, Larry. 1994. "Rethinking Civil Society: Toward Democratic Consolidation." *Journal of Democracy* 5(3): 4-17.

Diamond, Larry. 1995. *Promoting Democracy in the 1990s: Actors and Instruments, Issues and Imperatives*. Washington DC: Carnegie Commission on Preventing Deadly Conflict. <http://wwics.si.edu/subsites/ccpdc/pubs/di/fr.htm> (Accessed 15.11.07).

Diamond, Larry. 2003. "Can the Whole World Become Democratic? Democracy, Development, and International Policies." *Center for the Study of Democracy*. Irvine: University of California. <http://repositories.cdlib.org/csd/03-05> (Accessed 02.03.08).

Dilla, Harolodo and Philip Oxhorn. 2002. "The Virtues and Misfortunes of Civil Society in Cuba." *Latin American Perspectives* 29(4): 11-30.

Dobriansky, Paula J. 2003. "Democracy Promotion." *Foreign Affairs*, May/June. <http://www.foreignaffairs.org/20030501faresponse11226/paula-j-dobriansky-thomas-carothers /democracy-promotion.html> (Accessed 05.11.07).

Domínguez, Jorge I. 1978. *Cuba: Order and Revolution*. London: The Belknap Press.

Domínguez, Jorge I. 2000. "An Increasingly Civil Cuba." Review of *Looking at Cuba: Essays on Culture* and *Civil Society*, by Rafael Hernández; *Social Participation: Urban and Community Development*, by Aurora Vázquez Penelas and Roberto Dávalos Domínguez (eds.). *Foreign Policy* 120: 100-102.

Drezner, Daniel W. 2000. "The Complex Causation of Sanction Outcomes." In Steve Chan and A. Cooper Drury (eds.). *Sanctions as Economic Statecraft: Theory and Practice*. London: Macmillian Press: 213-233.

Fisk, Daniel W. 2002. "Initiative for a New Cuba: Address by Deputy Assistant Secretary Daniel W. Fisk before the National Summit on Cuba." *State Department Press Release*. Sept. 17. <http://www.state.gov/p/wha/ci/13525.htm> (Accessed 15.08.08).

Fox News. 2003. "U.S. aid to Cuban dissidents may do more harm than good." Apr. 13. <http://www.foxnews.com/story/0,2933,84057,00.html> (Accessed 05.08.08).

Freedom House. 2007. *The Worst of the Worst: The World's Most Repressive Societies 2007*. New York: Freedom House. <http://www.freedomhouse.org/uploads /special_report/58.pdf> (Accessed 12.08.08).

Friedman, Douglas. 2004. *Civil Society in Contemporary Cuba: U.S. Policy and the Cuban Reality*. Paper presented at the 2004 Southern Political Science Association Conference, New Orleans, LA, January 8-11.

Galtung, Johan. 1967. "On the Effects of International Economic Sanctions: With Examples from the Case of Rhodesia." *World Politics* 19(3): 378-416.

Geddes, Barbara. 1999. "What Do We Know About Democratization After Twenty Years?" *Annual Review of Political Science* 2: 115-144.

Gelbard, Robert S. 1992. "The Cuban Democracy Act and US policy toward Cuba – Statement by Principal Deputy Assistant Secretary For Inter-American Affairs Robert S. Gelbard." *Department of State Dispatch*. Aug. 17. <http://findarticles. com/p/articles/mi_m1584/is_n33_v3/ai_12686837/pg_2> (Accessed 24.04.08).

Gershman, Carl and Michael Allen. 2006. "The Assault on Democracy Assistance." *Journal of Democracy* 17(2): 36-51.

Goodman, Walter. 1992. "Review/television: Cuban exiles and U.S. policy on Castro." *New York Times*. Oct. 14. <http://www.nytimes.com/1992/10/14/ movies/review-television-cuban-exiles-and-us-policy-on-castro.html> (Accessed 22.07.08).

Goodnough, Abby. 2006. "U.S. pushes anti-Castro TV, but is anyone watching?" *New York Times*. Sept. 27. <http://www.nytimes.com/2006/09/27/us/27marti. html?n=Top/Reference/Times%20Topics/Subjects/C/Cuban-Americans> (Accessed 08.08.08).

Granma International. 2008. "Cuba demands answers from United States regarding activities of Interests Section in Havana." May 22. <http://www.granma.cu/ INGLES/2008/mayo/juev22/felipe.html> (Accessed 05.25.08).

Gratius, Susanne 2001. "Das Verhältnis Europa – Kuba: Der Antagonismus zwischen wirtschaftlicher Annäherung und politischer Distanz." In Ottmar Ette and Martin Franzbach (eds.). *Kuba heute: Politik, Wirtschaft, Kultur*. Frankfurt am Main: Vervuert: 193-219.

Griswold, Daniel T. 2002. *No: The Embargo Harms Cubans and Gives Castro and Excuse for the Policy Failures of His Regime*. May 27. Washington DC: Cato Institute. <http://www.cato.org/current/globalization/pubs/griswold020527. html> (Accessed 25.06.08).

Haass, Richard N. and Meghan L. O'Sullivan. 2000. "Terms of Engagement: Alternative to Punitive Policies." *Survival* 42(2): 113-135.

Haney, Patrick J. and Walt Vanderbush. 1999. "The Role of Ethnic Interest Groups in U.S. Foreign Policy: The Case of the Cuban American National Foundation." *International Studies Quarterly* 43: 341-361.

Hawkins, Dale. 2001. "Democratization Theory and Nontransitions: Insights from Cuba." *Comparative Politics* 33(4): 441-461.

Hoffmann, Bert. 2001a. "Außenpolitik, internationale Beziehungen und das Verhältnis zu den USA: Veränderungen und Kontinuitäten seit 1989." In Ottmar Ette und Martin Franzbach (eds.). *Kuba heute: Politik, Wirtschaft, Kultur.* Frankfurt am Main: Vervuert: 153-191.

Hoffmann, Bert. 2001b. "Transformation and Continuity in Cuba." *Review of Radical Political Economics* 33(1): 1-20.

Hoffmann, Bert and Laurence Whitehead. 2006. "Cuban Exceptionalism Revisited." *GIGA Working Paper,* 28. Hamburg: German Institute of Global and Area Studies. <http://www.giga-hamburg.de/index.php?file=workingpapers.html& folder=publikationen> (Accessed 24.02.08).

Holmes, Steven A. and Lizette Alvarez. 2000. "Senate approves easing sanctions on food to Cuba." *New York Times.* October 19. <http://www.nytimes.com/2000/ 10/19/world/senate-approves-easing-sanctions-on-food-to-cuba.html?scp=10& sq=agriculture%2C+cuba&st=nyt> (Accessed (17.08.09).

Hufbauer, Gary Clyde, Jeffrey J. Schott and Kimberly Ann Elliott. 1985. *Economic Sanctions Reconsidered.* Washington DC: Institute for International Economics.

Hunt, Michael H. 1987. *Ideology and U.S. Foreign Policy.* New Haven: Yale University Press.

Huntington, Samuel P. 1991. *The Third Wave: Democratization in the Late Twentieth Century.* Oklahoma: University of Oklahoma Press.

Kennedy, Robert. 1963. *Memorandum for Honorable Dean Rusk Secretary of State; RE: Travel To Cuba.* Washington DC: The National Security Archive. <http://www.gwu.edu/~nsarchiv/NSAEBB/NSAEBB158/index.htm> (Accessed 04.06.08).

Linz, Juan J. and Alfred Stepan. 1996. *Problems of Democratic Transition and Consolidation: Southern Europe, South American and Post-Communist Countries.* Baltimore: The Johns Hopkins University Press.

Lipset, Seymour Martin. 1959. "Some Social Requisites of Democracy: Economic Development and Political Legitimacy." *The American Political Science Review* 53: 69-105.

Londregan, John B. and Keith T. Poole. 1990. "Poverty, the Coup Trap, and the Seizure of Executive Power." *World Politics* 42(2): 151-183.

Lowe, David. 2008. "Idea to Reality: A Brief History of the National Endowment for Democracy." *The National Endowment for Democracy.* <http://www.ned.org/ about/nedhistory.html#1> (Accessed 05.04.08).

Luscombe, Richard. 2006. "Cuban democracy funds spent on game boys." *Guardian Unlimited.* Nov. 15. <http://www.guardian.co.uk/world/2006/nov/15/cuba. richardluscombe> (Accessed 12.03.08).

Lutjens, Sheryl L. 2006. "National Security, the State and the Politics of U.S.-Cuba Educational Exchange." *Latin American Perspectives* 33: 58-80.

Mansfeldová, Zdenka and Máté Szabó. 2000. "Zivilgesellschaft im Transformationsprozeß Ost-Mitteleuropas: Ungarn, Polen und die Tschechoslowakei." In Wolfgang Merkel (ed.). *Systemwechsel 5: Zivilgesellschaft und Transformation.* Opladen: Leske & Budrich: 89-114.

Marino, Soraya Castro. 2006. "The Bush Administration and Academic and Educational Exchange Between Cuba and the United States." *Latin American Perspectives* 33: 13-28.

Marinov, Nikolay. 2005. "Do Economic Sanctions Destabilize Country Leaders?" *American Journal of Political Science* 49(3): 564-576.

Martin, John Bartlow. 1978. *U.S. Policy in the Caribbean*. Boulder: Westview Press.

Martínez, Milagros. 2006. "Academic Exchange Between Cuba and the United States: A Brief Overview." *Latin American Perspectives* 33: 29-42.

McKinley, William. 1898. "Message to the Congress of the United States, April 11, 1898." In Henry Steele Commager (ed.). 1973. *Documents of American History: Volume II, Since 1898*. Ninth edn. New Jersey: Prentice-Hall: 1-4.

McKinley, James C. Jr. 2008. "Raúl Castro gives signals that Cuba will change." *New York Times*. Dec. 6. <http://www.nytimes.com/2008/02/26/world/americas/26iht-cuba.5.10447099.html?pagewanted=1&_r=1> (Accessed 02.05.09).

McKinley, James C. Jr. 2007. "For U.S. exporters in Cuba, business trumps politics." *New York Times*. Nov. 12. <http://www.nytimes.com/2007/11/12/world/americas/12cuba.html> (Accessed 28.07.08).

Mercer, Claire. 2002. "NGOs, Civil Society and Democratization: A Critical Review of the Literature." *Progress in Development Studies* 2(1): 5-22.

Merkel, Wolfgang. 1999. *Systemtransformation: Eine Einführung in die Theorie und Empirie der Transformationsforschung*. Opladen: Leske & Budrich.

Merkel, Wolfgang and Hans-Joachim Lauth. 1998. "Systemwechsel und Zivilgesellschaft: Welche Zivilgesellschaft braucht die Demokratie?" *Aus Politik und Zeitgeschichte* B 6-7/98: 3-12.

Mesa-Lago, Carmelo. 2007. "The Cuban Economy in 2006-2007." In *Cuba In Transition: Volume 17*. Washington DC: Association for the Study of the Cuban Economy: 1-20.

Monroe, James. 1823. "Message of President James Monroe at the Commencement of the First Session of the 18th Congress, December 2, 1823." *U.S. National Archives*. Presidential Messages of the 18th Congress. Record Group 46, Records of the United States Senate, 1789-1990. <http://www.ourdocuments.gov/doc.php?doc=23&page=transcript> (Accessed 25.03.08).

National Endowment for Democracy. 2006. *The Backlash Against Democracy Assistance*. Washington DC: National Endowment For Democracy. <http://www.ned.org/publications/reports/backlash06.pdf> (Accessed 15.11.07).

National Endowment for Democracy. 2008. *Strengthening Democracy Abroad: The Role of the National Endowment for Democracy*. <http://www.ned.org/about/principlesObjectives.html> (Accessed 05.04.08).

NBC6. 2006. "Report: Ros-Lehtinen did call for Castro's assassination." Dec. 23. <http://www.nbc6.net/news/10598324/detail.html> (Accessed 28.07.08).

Obama, Barack. 2007. "Our Main Goal: Freedom in Cuba." *Miami Herald,* Aug. 21.

O'Donnell, Guillermo and Philippe C. Schmitter. 1986. *Transitions from Authoritarian Rule: Tentative Conclusions about Uncertain Democracies*. Baltimore: The Johns Hopkins University Press.

Pape, Robert A. 1997. "Why Economic Sanctions Do Not Work." *International Security* 22(2): 90-136.

Parsons, Claudia. 2007. "U.N. votes against U.S. embargo on Cuba for 16th year." *Reuters*. Oct. 30. <http://www.reuters.com/article/newsOne/idUSN3016064020 071030> (Accessed 13.11.07).

Paxton, Pamela. 2002. "Social Capital and Democracy: An Interdependent Relationship." *American Sociological Review* 67(2): 254-277.

Pearson, Ruth and Vivienne Lewis. 1995. "NGOs and Cuba: Opportunity or Opportunism?" *Development in Practice* 5(1): 16-25.

Pérez, Louis A. Jr. 1999. "Incurring a Debt of Gratitude: 1898 and the Moral Sources of United States Hegemony in Cuba." *The American Historical Review* 104(2): 356-398.

Pérez, Louis A. Jr. 2002. "Fear and Loathing of Fidel Castro: Sources of US Policy Toward Cuba." *Journal of Latin American Studies* 34: 227-254.

Pérez Roque, Felipe. 2003. *Press conference by Foreign Minister of the Republic of Cuba, Felipe Pérez Roque on the mercenaries at the service of the empire who stood trial on April 3,4,5 and 7, 2003.* Havana, Apr. 9. Via Canadian Network on Cuba. <http://www.canadiannetworkoncuba.ca/Documents/Roque-Dissidents-Apr03.shtml> (Accessed 05.08.08).

Peterson, Merrill D. (ed.). 1984. *Thomas Jefferson: Writings.* United States: The Library of America.

Petras, James and Morris Morely. 1996. "Clinton's Cuba Policy: Two Steps Backward, One Step Forward." *Third World Quarterly* 17(2): 269-287.

Preeg, Ernest H. 1997. *The Helms-Burton Law and U.S. Interests in the World Trade Organization: Testimony Before the House Committee on International Relations, Subcommittee on International Economic Policy and Trade.* March 19. Washington DC: Center For Strategic and International Studies. <http://www.csis.org/component/option,com_csis_congress/task,view/id,15/> (Accessed 15.02.08).

Prensa Latina. 2007. "Claims and evictions in U.S. plan for Cuba." July 21. <http://www.cubavsbloqueo.cu/Default.aspx?tabid=348> (Accessed 22.06.08).

Przeworski, Adam and Fernando Limongi. 1997. "Modernization: Theories and Facts." *World Politics* 49: 155-183.

Przeworski, Adam, Michael Alvarez, José Antonio Cheibub and Fernando Limongi. 1997. "What Makes Democracies Endure?" In Larry Diamond, Marc F. Plattner, Yun-han Chu and Hung-mao Tien (eds.). *Consolidating the Third Wave Democracies: Themes and Perspectives.* Baltimore MD: The Johns Hopkins University Press: 295-311.

Pumar, Enrique S. 1999. "The Internal Opposition and Civil Society: An Assessment." In *Cuba in Transition Volume 9.* Silver Spring MD: Association for the Study of the Cuban Economy: 368-377.

Reagan, Ronald. 1982. "Address to Members of the British Parliament June 8 1982." *The Public Papers of President Ronald W. Reagan.* Ronald Reagan Presidential Library. <http://www.reagan.utexas.edu/archives/speeches/1982/60882a.htm> (Accessed 28.07.08).

Reagan, Ronald. 1983. "Address to the Nation on Events in Lebanon and Grenada October 27 1983." *The Presidential Papers of President Ronald W. Reagan.* Ronald Reagan Presidential Library. <http://www.reagan.utexas.edu/archives/speeches/1983/102783b.htm> (Accessed 20.05.09).

Republic of Cuba. Ministry of Foreign Affairs. 2008a. *Bush's Anti-Cuban Plan*. <http://embacu.cubaminrex.cu/Default.aspx?tabid=7419> (Accessed 02.06.08).

Republic of Cuba. Ministry of Foreign Affairs. 2008b. *The Cuban Political and Electoral System*. <http://www.cubaminrex.cu/English/61CDH/Cuba%B4s%20Political%20and%20election%20System.htm> (Accessed 14.08.08).

Richter, Paul. 2008. "Cuba USAID program gets overhaul." *Los Angeles Times*. May 7. <http://www.latimes.com/news/nationworld/washingtondc/la-fg-uscuba7-20 08may07,0,6311240.story> (Accessed 28.07.08).

Rohter, Larry. 1992. "A rising Cuban-American leader: statesman to some, bully to others." *New York Times*. Oct. 29. <http://www.nytimes.com/1992/10/29/us/a-rising-cuban-american-leader-statesman-to-some-bully-to-others.html?page wanted=1> (Accessed 22.06.08).

San Martin, Nancy. 2004. "U.S. Treasury OFAC has 6 times more personnel on Cuba than Bin Laden." *Miami Herald*. May 1. Via Havana Journal. <http://havanajournal.com/politics/entry/us_treasury_ofac_has_6_times_more_personn el_on_cuba_than_bin_laden/> (Accessed 02.07.08).

Sanchez, Ray. 2008. "More details released on U.S. Interests chief, Miami support to dissidents." *The South Florida Sun-Sentinel*. May 20. Via Center for International Policy. <http://ciponline.org/cuba/cubainthenews/052008MoreDetails Released.htm> (Accessed 04.08.08).

Schmitter, Philippe C. 1997. "Civil Society East and West." In Larry Diamond, Marc F. Plattner, Yun-han Chu and Hung-mao Tien (eds.). *Consolidating the Third Wave Democracies: Themes and Perspectives*. Baltimore: The Johns Hopkins University Press: 135-159.

Schoultz, Lars. 2002. "Blessings of Liberty: The United States and the Promotion of Democracy in Cuba." *Journal of Latin American Studies* 34(2): 397-425.

Schreiber, Anna P. 1973. "Economic Coercion as an Instrument of Foreign Policy: U.S. Economic Measures Against Cuba and the Dominican Republic." *World Politics* 25(3): 387-413.

Smis, Stefan and Kim van der Borght. 1999. "The EU-U.S. Compromise on the Helms-Burton and D'Amato Acts." *The American Journal of International Law* 93(1): 227-236.

Smith, Mark S. 2009. "Obama heads to Americas Summit with Cuba focus." *ABC News*. April 17. <http://abcnews.go.com/International/wireStory?id=7359465> (Accessed on 02.05.09).

Staten, Clifford L.. 2003. *The History of Cuba*. New York: Palgrave Macmillian.

Sweig, Julia E. 2007. "Fidel's Final Victory." *Foreign Affairs* 86(1): 39-56.

United Nations Development Programme. 2007. *Human Development Report 2007/ 2008*. New York: Palgrave Macmillan.

U.S. Agency for International Development. 2005. *USAID Cuba Program*. Nov. 5. <http://pdf.usaid.gov/pdf_docs/PDACH738.pdf> (Accessed 02.05.08).

U.S. Agency for International Development. 2006. *USAID/Cuba Operational Plan FY 2006*. June. <http://pdf.usaid.gov/pdf_docs/PDACH412.pdf> (Accessed 02.05.08).

U.S. Commission for Assistance to a Free Cuba. 2004. *Report to the President*. May.

U.S. Commission for Assistance to a Free Cuba. 2006a. *Report to the President*. July.

U.S. Commission for Assistance to a Free Cuba. 2006b. *CAFC: Implementation Highlights*. July 20.   <http://www.cafc.gov/cafc/rls/69299.htm> (Accessed 14.06.08).

U.S. Commission for Assistance to a Free Cuba. 2006c. *Compact with the People of Cuba*. July 10.   <http://www.cafc.gov/cafc/rpt/2006/68746.htm> (Accessed 15.11.07).

U.S. Commission for Assistance to a Free Cuba. 2007. *Mission and Members*. <http://www.cafc.gov/mission/> (Accessed 15.11.07).

U.S. Congress. 1898. "Joint Resolution of April 20." In Henry Steele Commager (ed.). 1973. *Documents of American History: Volume II, Since 1898*. Ninth edn. New Jersey: Prentice-Hall: 5.

U.S. Congress. 1996. *Cuban Liberty and Democratic Solidarity (Libertad) Act of 1996*. H.R. 927. 104th Cong., 2nd sess. Washington DC: Government Printing Office. <http://www.ustreas.gov/offices/enforcement/ofac/legal/statutes/libertad .pdf> (Accessed 08.02.08).

U.S. Congressional Research Service. 2005. *Cuba: Issues for the 109th Congress*. Report No. RL32730. Jan. 13. By Mark P. Sullivan. <http://digital.library.unt. edu/govdocs/crs/permalink/meta-crs-6250> (Accessed 02.03.08).

U.S. Congressional Research Service. 2006. *Cuba: U.S. Restrictions on Travel and Remittances*. Report No. RL31139. Aug. 30. By Mark P. Sullivan. <http://digital.library.unt.edu/govdocs/crs/permalink/meta-crs-9812> (Accessed 02.03.08).

U.S.-Cuba Trade and Economic Council. 2008. *Economic Eye on Cuba, March 2008*. <http://www.cubatrade.org> (Accessed 28.07.08).

U.S. Department of State. 1952. *Foreign Relations of the United States: Diplomatic Papers 1933, Volume V, The American Republics*. Washington DC: U.S. Government Printing Office.

U.S. Department of State. 1983. *Foreign Relations of the United States, 1952-1954: Volume IV, The American Republics*. Washington DC: Government Printing Office.

U.S. Department of State. 1991. *Foreign Relations of the United States, 1958-1960: Volume VI, Cuba*. Washington DC: U.S. Government Printing Office.

U.S. Department of State. 1996. *Foreign Relations of the United States, 1961-1963: Volume XI, Cuban Missile Crisis and Aftermath*. Washington DC: U.S. Government Printing Office.

U.S. Department of State. 1997. *Foreign Relations of the United States, 1961-1963: Volume X, Cuba 1961-1962*. Washington DC: U.S. Government Printing Office.

U.S. Department of State. 2005. *Foreign Relations of the United States, 1964-1968: Volume XXXII, Dominican Republic; Cuba; Haiti; Guyana*. Washington DC: U.S. Government Printing Office.

U.S. Department of State 2006. *Second Report of the Commission for Assistance to a Free Cuba and the Compact With the Cuban People. Briefing with Secretary of Commerce Carlos Gutierrez and Cuba Transition Coordinator Caleb McCarry*. July 10.   <http://www.state.gov/secretary/rm/2006/68776.htm> (Accessed 15.08.08).

U.S. Department of State and Agency for International Development. 2007. *Foreign Operations Congressional Budget Justification: Foreign Operations Fiscal Year 2008.* <http://www.state.gov/documents/organization/84462.pdf> (Accessed 15.02.08).

U.S. Department of State and Broadcasting Board of Governors. Office of Inspector General. 2003. *Review of the Effectiveness and Implantation of Office of Cuba Broadcasting's New Program Initiatives.* Report No. IBO-A-03-01. Jan. <http://oig.state.gov/documents/organization/17948.pdf> (Accessed 16.08.08).

U.S. Department of State and Broadcasting Board of Governors. Office of Inspector General. 2007. *Report of Inspection, Office of Cuba Broadcasting.* Report No. ISP-IB-07-35, June. <http://oig.state.gov/documents/organization/89909.pdf> (Accessed 16.08.08).

U.S. Department of Treasury. Office of Foreign Assets Control. 2004a. *An Overview of the Cuban Assets Control Regulations Title 31 Part 515 of the U.S. Code of Federal Regulations.* <http://www.ustreas.gov/offices/enforcement/ofac/ programs/cuba/cuba.pdf> (Accessed 08.06.08).

U.S. Department of Treasury. Office of Foreign Assets Control. 2004b. *Recent OFAC Actions.* June 16. <http://www.treas.gov/offices/enforcement/ofac/ actions/20040616.html> (Accessed .08.06.08).

U.S. Department of Treasury. Office of Foreign Assets Control. 2005. *Terrorist Assets Report: Calendar Year 2005.* <http://www.treas.gov/offices/enforcement /ofac/reports/tar2005.pdf> (Accessed 16.06.08).

U.S. Department of Treasury. Office of Foreign Assets Control. 2008a. *Enforcement Information for May 2, 2008.* <http://www.treas.gov/offices/enforcement/ofac/ civpen/penalties/05292008.pdf> (Accessed 08.06.08).

U.S. Department of Treasury. Office of Foreign Assets Control. 2008b. *Enforcement Information for June 6, 2008.* <http://www.treas.gov/offices/enforcement/ofac/ civpen/penalties/06062008.pdf> (Accessed 21.06.08).

U.S. Department of The Treasury. Office of Public Affairs. 2004. *Treasury Secretary John W. Snow Remarks to Cuban American Leaders, Miami, FL.* Feb. 9. <http://www.treas.gov/press/releases/js1160.htm> (Accessed 28.06.08).

U.S. Government Accountability Office. 2006. *U.S. Democracy Assistance for Cuba Needs Better Management and Oversight.* Nov. Report No. GAO-07-147. <http://pdf.usaid.gov/pdf_docs/PCAAB525.pdf> (Accessed 15.02.08).

U.S. Government. White House. 2009. "Fact Sheet: Reaching Out to the Cuban People." *Office of the Press Secretary.* April 13. <http://www.whitehouse.gov/ the_press_office/Fact-Sheet-Reaching-out-to-the-Cuban-people/> (Accessed 03.05.09).

U.S. House of Representatives. 2007a. "The Department of State, Foreign Operations and Related Programs Appropriations Act, 2008." 110th Cong., 1st sess. *Congressional Record* 153(101). June 21: H6833. <http://frwebgate. access.gpo. gov/cgi-bin/getpage.cgi?position=all&page=H6833&dbname=2007_record> (Accessed on 15.02.08).

U.S. House of Representatives. 2007b. *Free Trade With Cuba Act.* H.R.624. 110th Cong. 1st sess. Jan. 22. Washington DC: U.S. Government Printing Office. <http://frwebgate.access.gpo.gov/cgi-bin/getdoc.cgi?dbname=110_cong_bills& docid=f:h624ih.txt.pdf> (Accessed 23.08.08).

U.S. House of Representatives. Committee on Appropriations. 2008. *Consolidated Appropriations Act, 2008*. H.R. 2764. 110th Cong., 1st sess. Washington DC: Government Printing Office. <http://www.gpoaccess.gov/congress/house/appropriations/08conappro.html> (Accessed 20.0808).

U.S. House of Representatives. Committee on International Relations. 2006. *Report of the Commission for Assistance to a Free Cuba*. Hearing, July 27. 109th Cong., 2nd sess. Washington DC: U.S. Government Printing Office. <http://commdocs.house.gov/committees/intlrel/hfa28969.000/hfa28969_0f.htm> (Accessed 10.06.08).

U.S. House of Representatives. Select Committee on Assassinations. 1979. *Investigation of the Assassination of President John F. Kennedy, Vol. IV*. Sept. 22, 25 and 26, 1978. 95th Cong., 2nd sess. Washington DC: Government Printing Office.

U.S. National Security Council. 1977. *Presidential Directive/NSC-6*. March 15. Washington DC: The National Security Archive. <http://www.gwu.edu/~nsarchiv/NSAEBB/NSAEBB269/index.htm> (Accessed on 17.07.09).

U.S. National Security Council. 2006. *The National Security Strategy of the United States of America*. March. <http://www.whitehouse.gov/nsc/nss/2006/> (Accessed 11.02.08).

U.S. Senate. Select Committee to Study Governmental Operations with Respect to Intelligence Activities. 1975. *Alleged Assassination Plots Involving Foreign Leaders*. Nov. 20. 94th Cong., 1st sess. Washington DC: U.S. Government Printing Office.

U.S. Senate. Committee on Foreign Relations. 2003. *Challenges For U.S. Policy Toward Cuba*. Hearing, Oct. 2. 108th Cong., 1st sess. Washington DC: U.S. Government Printing Office. <http://frwebgate.access.gpo.gov/cgi-bin/getdoc.cgi?dbname=108_senate_hearings&docid=f:91684.pdf> (Accessed 11.12.07).

U.S. Trade Sanctions and Export Reform Act of 2000. Title 22 U.S. Code, Ch. 79, Sec. 7207-7211.

Weissert, Will. 2007. "Cuba: US embargo has cost over $89B." *Associated Press*. Sept. 18. Via CubaNet. <http://www.cubanet.org/Cnews/y07/sep07/20e11.htm> (Accessed 28.06.08).

Weissert, Will. 2009. "Raul Castro: Obama's Cuba policy changes 'minimal'" *ABC News*. April 29. <http://abcnews.go.com/International/wireStory?id=7459436> (Accessed 02.05.09).

Whitehead, Laurence. 1986. "International Aspects of Democratization." In Guillermo O'Donnell, Philippe C. Schmitter, and Laurence Whitehead (eds.). *Transitions from Authoritarian Rule: Comparative Perspectives*. Baltimore: The Johns Hopkins University Press: 3-46.

Whitehead, Laurence. 2002. "The Imposition of Democracy: The Caribbean." In Laurence Whitehead (ed.). *The International Dimensions of Democratization: Europe and the Americas*. Oxford: Oxford University Press: 59-92.

Wiktorowicz, Quintan. 2000. "Civil Society as Social Control: State Power in Jordan." *Comparative Politics* 33(1): 43-61.

Williams, William A. (ed.). 1972. *The Shaping of American Diplomacy*. Chicago: Rand Mcnally & Co.

Academic must-reads